AMMA

To
DIVINE MOTHER
in all Her many manifestations

Amma's blessing in Malaylam
Translation:
Om
May the lives of my darling children
become a celebration.
Love and kisses for my children.

AMMA
A LIVING SAINT

JUDITH CORNELL

PIATKUS

✿ Visit the Piatkus website! ✿

Piatkus publishes a wide range of exciting fiction and non-fiction,
including books on health, mind body & spirit, sex, self-help, cookery,
biography and the paranormal. If you want to:

- read descriptions of our popular titles

- buy our books over the internet

- take advantage of our special offers

- enter our monthly competition

- learn more about your favourite Piatkus authors

visit our website at:

www.piatkus.co.uk

CONTENTS

ACKNOWLEDGMENTS

I would like to thank Amma's parents, Sugunanandan and Damayanti, and the numerous men and women from all over the world who shared their experiences of Amma with me. Many of their firsthand accounts were woven together with various other archival resources to create Amma's life story.

I am deeply grateful to Swami Paramatmananda, Steve Fleisher, and Bhakti Guest, board members of the Mata Amritanandamayi Center (MA), in San Ramon, California, for allowing me complete access to photos, videos, magazine and newspaper articles, and books, including an earlier biography published in India by the Amritapuri Ashram. Originally it was written in Malayalam, by Professor M. Ramakrishnan Nair and later translated into English and rewritten by Swami Amritaswarupananda.

I would especially like to thank the following monastics of the Amritapuri Ashram in India: Swami Jnanamritananda for help in arranging interviews in India; Brahmachari Shubamrita for his gifts of translating; and Brahmachari Anubhavamrita for rendering into English a complicated Malayalam text and Brahmachari Shantamrita for help in arranging a visit to the Amrita Institutes of Technology. To Swami Amritaswarupananda,

Swami Ramakrishnananda, Dr. Neelakantan Namboodiri, Brahmachari Dayamrita, Swamini Amritaprana, and Swamini Krishnamritaprana for their invaluable comments and help as the manuscript unfolded. A special thanks to Dr. I. C. Dave for arranging a special interview with his friends Dr. I. V. V. Raghavacharyulu and Dr. Srivastava of the Babha Atomic Research Centre in Bombay. And to Dr. Srivastava for his graciousness in hosting the occasion.

Also special thanks to Shawn Brinsfield and Steven Silberfein for access to their unpublished notes and video transcripts of interviews with Amma's parents, grandmother, brothers and sisters, and local villagers. And to George Brunswig for his help in the initial stages of archival research. And to: Corey Kilgannon, of the *New York Times,* for allowing me to use his unpublished material; Sabine Chaloupy from France, for her help in gathering photos, permissions, and translating stories from French into English; and Mardi Muller and Case Rienstra from the Netherlands, who shared their journalistic expertise.

A heartfelt thanks to: Eileen Cope, my literary agent; Joann Davis, my editor; China Galland and Jean Shinoda Bolen, M.D., who supported this project from the beginning. And to Elsa Dixon for her expertise in helping me to craft Amma's story in a dynamic way, and Layla Smith for the great work transcribing the interviews.

I owe a special debt of gratitude to the following friends and colleagues who helped in various ways by giving valuable feedback on all or parts of the manuscript: Elizabeth Rothenburger, Don Campbell, Dr. Michael Flanagin of the C. G. Jung Institute in San Francisco, Dr. Jim Ryan, cochair of Asian and Comparative Studies, at the California Institute of Integral Studies, Dr. David Frawley, director of the American Institute of Vedic Sciences, Dr. William Gough, president of the Foundation for Mind-Being Research, Georgia Kelly, Marilena Scott, Janani, Hari Sudha, Louise Pare, Judy Walter, Olga Luchakova, M.D.,

Ph.D., Carolyn Pincus, Paul Kelly, Linda and Robert Knickerbocker, Robert and Sharona Jepson, Susan Sopcak, Candice Furhman, and Ron Gottsegen.
I take full responsibility for any errors that remain.

A percentage of all royalties from the sale of this book go to the Mata Amritanandamayi Center (MA Center) in support of Amma's charities.

AMMA

PROLOGUE

New York City, July 15, 1999

Police officers William La Pough and Juan Colon were driving their unmarked patrol car through Central Park at 12:45 A.M. They found the park, like the tepid night air, to be quiet and tranquil. As they drove up Central Park West and passed the Museum of Natural History, they saw a large group of shoeless people dressed in white who were congregating outside the Universalist Church on the corner of West Seventy-sixth street. In New York this can only mean one thing: homeless people, so the officers decided to stop.

"What's going on?" they asked the people who were standing outside the church.

The people explained that Amma, a greatly respected saint from a poor remote village in southern India, was in New York City as part of her yearly world tour to the United States. "As a way of blessing people, Amma gives hugs of unconditional love. In the last three days she has given thousands of hugs to people coming to this Universalist Church," one man told them. This was Amma's last night in the city before finishing the tour in Boston and Rhode Island. Curious, the officers decided to look inside. William and Juan stepped into a mass of people jammed into a church too small to hold them. Once inside, they heard the melodious and joyful sounds of sacred South Indian chants—chants composed by Amma herself. Amma's monastic order, dressed in the traditional orange robes of monks (swamis), along with a few other nonmonastic adults and children on the tour, were sitting cross-legged on the floor near the front of the church, playing various musical instruments and singing.

Steve Fleisher, the lawyer for Amma's nonprofit spiritual organization, noticed the officers and asked if they would like to get a blessing from Amma. After assuring them they would not have to wait in the long line, they said that they would. Steve guided the officers to the front of the altar where Amma was sitting in a chair, hugging people. On this special occasion called Devi Bhava, in the rich tradition of East Indian spirituality that honors the feminine aspect of God, she was dressed in the regal manner of a Hindu goddess, wearing a beautiful silk sari with elaborate gold trim, and a silver crown on her head.

New York Times reporter Corey Kilgannon, a young man in his early thirties, had arrived at the church many hours earlier on his way home from work. He said that he felt spiritually bankrupt and had come to the church that night as a skeptic with the specific purpose of debunking the myth of Amma and her hugs. He was aware that the year before, in July 1998, the *New York Times* had done a full-page spread on her, as had other major national newspapers. In that interview Amma had told a reporter, "I always wanted to know the cause of misery and thought if sorrow is a truth, then there must be a cause and a way out. I realize my purpose is to console—to personally wipe away tears through selfless love, compassion, and service."

Corey, with hopes of getting a story, joined the long lines of people sitting cross-legged on the tile floor, inching their way up the middle aisle of the church toward the altar, where Amma hugged all comers.

He said, "Everyone held gifts for Amma, and things for her to sign, from photographs to Hallmark cards to candy bars. The guy next to me was a cab driver who wanted his air freshener blessed. After I got my hug from Amma I sat nearby on the stage to get a mantra (holy name of God) from her.

"But suddenly, the crowd of thousands of kneeling supplicants—who had been entranced, chanting for hours—suddenly burst into applause. Two policemen, in full uniform, wearing nine-millimeter guns and bulletproof vests, and badges, were climbing the altar toward Amma.

"New York City at this time was being led by Mayor Rudolph Giuliani, a Catholic school–bred Republican politician who gained a reputation for cracking down on anything resembling deviant behavior, and giving broad license to the police to be the same way. Rescuing New York City from the criminals was good politics, and the law of the land essentially became: arrest first, ask questions later.

"My heart raced as I wondered if New York's Finest were actually going to handcuff the 'Hugging Saint.' Had the year's most bizarre news story suddenly fallen into my lap? Maybe a hug from Amma was paying early dividends for this ambitious, young reporter.

"But the officers never reached for the cuffs. Instead, they kneeled down before Amma, who, dressed in her silver crown and white sari, smiled broadly and pulled the burly officers to her chest and whispered her blessings into their ears. Rising, they got the customary rose petal and Hershey's chocolate kiss from Amma and another round of applause from the crowd.

"Smelling a humorous item for the *Times*'s society column, I zipped over to the officers to get a quote. As it turned out, it wasn't these cops' first brush with spirituality. Officer La Pough met

Mother Teresa during a New York visit, and Officer Colon guarded the pope in 1995.

"I've always noticed that New York City cops all seem to maintain a similar attitude and expression—a kind of protective firewall of emotional insulation they keep just to survive and to maintain their sanity in this crazy city. Now, I'm no romantic. However, for a brief time after their encounter with Amma, these officers, in their stocking feet, holding their rose petals, seemed to lose that look. But with a pesky reporter bugging them for their names and a comment for the paper, they soon retreated back behind that Blue Wall."

Neither officer, although visibly affected by Amma's hug, realized at that point that they had just been blessed by a woman who is revered as a living saint and sage by millions in her own country, and who has been credited with thousands of miracles by her devoted followers. Her official name, Mata Amritanandamayi, means Mother of Immortal Bliss. She is more commonly known as Ammachi or Amma (Mother).

Two years before, in March 1997, the prime minister of India had hosted Amma in New Delhi as a special guest of the state at a grand reception. She was given the prestigious Scroll of Honor by the chief minister of New Delhi, which was the first time that a woman spiritual leader had *ever* received this award. It had only been given to the Shankaracharyas (distinguished leaders of the ancient Hindu swami order of monks) and to the pope. She was being honored for many things—her spiritual strength and wisdom, her universal love and compassion, and her service to humanity. As part of her service to humanity, she has founded numerous schools and over two hundred ashrams, consecrated twelve temples, established a monastic order, built a state-of-the-art medical hospital, established orphanages, set up a monthly pension fund for fifty thousand destitute women, and is now building twenty-five thousand free homes for the poor. These many great achievements are even more astonishing when one considers that this wise and influential woman has only a fourth-grade education. Amma's life began in a poor, remote Indian fishing village, where she lived in poverty and suffered from extreme gender, religious, and color prejudice. Her metamorphosis from an uneducated and abused domestic servant to an internationally revered spiritual leader and powerful force for good in the world is one of the most remarkable stories of our time.

Part 1 tells the story of Amma's birth, her harrowing childhood of poverty and abuse, and her divine calling to alleviate the sufferings of humanity. Part 2 highlights her rise to prominence as a respected international religious leader and great humanitarian—as it has unfolded until now. Her story is woven together from author interviews and various other archival materials and references (see Notes, pp. 245–253).

The ancient Hindu Vedas teach that "time" and "space" are illusions of our physical senses—a "man-made" classification applied to a series of changes and movements in Nature. This Vedic philosophy appears to be deeply imprinted in the Indian psyche.

The poor fishing villagers in Kerala, where Amma grew up, work with the cycles of the seasons to know when the fish are available, and when they will have to travel down the coast to catch fish. They aren't necessarily concerned that we might call this day March 13, 1999, or this hour 11 A.M. They may know the year, but exact dates of events are immaterial to them. They are just interested in catching fish—unlike we urban Westerners, who continually look at the clock and can't leave home without our appointment books under our arms.

Thus when the villagers or Amma's parents could not give the exact dates or times, regarding events in her early life, they have been stated as approximations. For example, Chapter 3, Krishna Unveiled (1970–1975), shows in parenthesis the approximate time period covered.

I first met Amma in 1987, when she came to California on her first world tour. As a religious skeptic, I carefully observed her over the next eleven years. During that period she grew in stature as a respected religious leader. By the eleventh year I tried to analyze what she was doing through her simple act of giving a loving hug to so many thousands, and it boggled my Western mind. How could any human do what she was doing—hour after hour, day after day, year after year?

In January 1998, I decided it was time for me to write a third book, and began in earnest working on several book ideas vastly different from the one you are about to read. But although I wrote continuously for six months and prayed each day to be inspired, the sacred muse was utterly unresponsive. Many trees have to give up their lives for any book to go into print, and as a result, I have always felt a deep spiritual and ecological accountability. Therefore, I could only be satisfied with a book I knew to be truly inspired and beneficial to humanity.

One morning in the middle of June, while deeply meditating, I once more desperately pleaded to God to inspire me with the writing. And then it happened! Amma's face came clearly into my mind and the sacred muse made it known beyond a doubt that this was the story I was to write.

On December 31, 1998, I embarked on a three-month pilgrimage to India to learn more about Amma and to acquire a dispassionate understanding of the tropical village life, to interview the people, and to visit her charities and the places where her life first unfolded. However there is a saying that you cannot know a person unless you walk in their shoes. During the last six weeks of my stay in India I traveled with Amma on the 1999 North Indian tour. At that point, I dropped the objective, rational stance of the biographer and became fully engrossed as a spiritual pilgrim and a subjective participant, basically to gain a visceral understanding of the rigors of her life (see Chapter 14, Spiritual Boot Camp). The North Indian tour covered thousands of grueling miles to various cities where she gave her blessing (darshan) of healing hugs to hundreds of thousands of people. This life-changing experience greatly expanded my initial perceptions of Amma.

ARRIVING IN INDIA
January 4, 1999

My plane flew low over Kerala's shimmering tropical waterways, which were bordered by countless shade-giving palm trees. I had landed in Trivandrum near the southern-most tip of India. On the bumpy, three-hour cab ride to the Amritapuri Ashram, I wondered what it would be like to meet Amma's parents.

My first impression of South India was that it is a paradoxical mix of spirituality and materialism. From the cab window, I was surprised to see posters of holy men next to graffiti of the hammer and sickle—symbol of the Communist Party of India. Later I learned that the CPI, a Marxist-influenced party, has ruled Kerala's coalition government since 1996.

When I arrived at the ashram, I learned that Amma had left the day before for Calicut, and wouldn't be back for a week. I decided to use that time to adjust to ashram life and to explore the village where she grew up. After registering at the office for foreign visitors, I wandered to the edge of the backwaters, along the eastern side of the ashram. On the way, I passed an older Indian couple sitting in plastic chairs outside a small, pale blue-green house. As I passed them, they motioned for me to come over to them.

Ferry boatman on the backwaters near Amritapuri Ashram.

The thought ran through my mind that perhaps these two might be Amma's parents. I had never seen a picture of them, but in our mutual attempt to communicate with each other through hand gestures, smiles, and our two entirely different languages, they confirmed for me that they were indeed Amma's parents. I found her father, Sugunanandan, with his big-bellied enthusiasm, to be dramatically extroverted, and her mother, Damayanti, to be much more contained, but radiant nonetheless.

The fact that they greeted me so pleasantly and with such goodwill was all the more remarkable, because they did not know I was their daughter's biographer. My first impression of Amma's parents was that they were truly authentic and loving people. I, however, wasn't prepared to see them so transformed.

Before arriving in India, I had already accomplished six months of research and had only known of Amma's parents through reading the older Indian biography. In that biography it graphically portrays the earlier years of Amma's life, at which time her parents *were* unloving and abusive.

Part 1

॰

EARLY LIFE AND CALLING

By seeking to know one's Self the Great Mother of all may be found. On finding the Mother, everything is found. Knowing the Mother means realizing the Mother, becoming Mother. Mā means "Atmā" (Self). "To become" actually means it ever is so.

ANANDAMAYI MĀ, BENGALI INDIAN SAGE (1896–1982)

Chapter 1

A LIGHT THAT IS BLACK
KERALA, LAND OF THE GODDESS (1934–1953)

Along the Malabar Coast, on the west side of South India, is the state of Kerala—a tropical landscape of unusual abundance and beauty. The land and air teem with wildlife and birds, and blackish gray sand beaches edge the warm waters of the Arabian Sea.

Kerala means "Place of Coconuts." Inland, palm, banana, coconut, cashew, and rubber trees thrive in the damp climate. Brilliant red hibiscus flowers blossom and are ritually offered by the Hindus to the goddess Kali—a goddess who has been worshipped in Kerala and all over India for thousands of years. The people of the region have a rich history of sacred drama and dance and are among the most industrious and well educated in the country.

Amma, born into a low caste, was the daughter of a fisherman. In the Quilon district of Kerala is Parayakadavu, a poor, small fishing village on a long, narrow island that is surrounded by the sea and brackish backwaters. For centuries, the families of Parayakadavu have made their living pulling fish from the sea. So it was with Amma's father's family, the Idamannels, who had fished the clear blue waters of the Arabian Sea for countless generations.

In addition to being fishermen, the men of the Idamannel family have also had a long tradition of charity. It has been their custom, after a hard day of fishing, to give away a portion of the catch to the villagers without accepting money in return. And after the sale of the rest of the catch, they would give away a few of these coins to the village children.

The tradition of charity and devout religious belief was evident in Amma's grandfather, Sri Velayudhan, a compassionate man and devout Hindu who was so ardent a believer in the ideal of ahimsa (not injuring) that he would not even allow a rat to be killed. Sri Velayudhan married Amma's grandmother, Srimati Madhavi, an equally devout and pious woman, whose practice it was (every morning from the time before her marriage and for the rest of her long life) to wake up before dawn and go to the family shrine room, where she would string garlands of flowers for the deities while chanting the Divine Names of God.

Fishing village where Amma was born
This picture of a group of fishermen, taken by the ashram in 1998, gives a sense of the timelessness in this remote village.

While such piety and deep spiritual belief are to be admired, they are by no means unusual in India. An Indian's spiritual beliefs affect his or her day-to-day life: governing thoughts, regulating actions, and providing a person with his or her sense of self—one's own "dharma," or personal course in life—much the same way a devout Jew or Christian's spiritual beliefs affect his or her life.

It is not surprising, then, that after being raised in an atmosphere of such piety and spirituality, Amma's father, Sugunanandan, the eldest son of Sri Velayudhan and Srimati Madhavi, should have ardent spiritual beliefs from an early age. As a small child, Amma's father became a faithful devotee of Lord Krishna, one of the most popular Hindu forms of God.

Sugunanandan began to practice the classic South Indian dance form of *Kathakali*, for which the region of Kerala is famous. In *Kathakali*, a troupe of male dancers in ornate makeup and costumes act out epic mythological tales of the gods and goddesses to the sound of pounding drums. During one performance Sugunanandan, who was playing Lord Krishna, reportedly became so deeply transcended into his character that he lost consciousness onstage.

Aside from these religious ecstasies, and the natural bustling activity of a family with five children, life at the Idamannel household was peaceful. The sound of the waves echoed gently from the nearby ocean. The grounds surrounding the house were lush with coconut and cashew trees, and the cashew nuts were a favorite snack of the Idamannel children.

One day after school, thirteen-year-old Sugunanandan and his cousin climbed a cashew tree to forage the branches for cashews, as they often did. Suddenly, through the branches of the tree, they saw a monk with long hair and a beard approaching the property. The boys were curious; in India, no stranger goes unnoticed, especially in the small villages. Not wanting to be seen, the boys sat motionless and quiet in the tree and watched as the monk roamed around the grounds of the house. Suddenly, he stopped and laughed, his face shining.

"I see many ascetics immersed in deep meditation in this place!" he cried out. "Many great souls lie under this ground, and many monks will achieve Liberation here. This will be a holy place!" He laughed again, and then continued his walking. Soon he was out of sight of the two astonished boys. The monk was never seen or heard from again.

This odd occurrence had been long forgotten when, as a grown man of twenty-one, Sugunanandan married Amma's mother, Damayanti, a young woman of twenty from the neighboring village of Bhandaraturuttu. Like her new husband, Damayanti had also been raised in an extremely pious and devout atmosphere. Her family even had its own family temple. She often fasted as part of her religious devotion, and she continued this practice into her married life.

Now with the new responsibilities of being a married man, Sugunanandan had to give up the *Kathakali* dance that he loved. Together, he and Damayanti raised a family and worked hard to make their living by marketing the fish he caught.

Before Amma's birth, Damayanti had two normal pregnancies. Before giving birth to her eldest daughter, Kasturi, and firstborn son, Subhagan, she was able to keep doing all her household chores during the whole nine months, after which her body would begin to swell. The swelling was a sign that her body was preparing to deliver.

At the news of Subhagan's birth, there was great rejoicing and celebration in both families. Sugunanandan made special trips to the temple to offer prayers of gratitude for this great gift of his firstborn son.

In India, the firstborn son is everything to the family. He will be the foundation on which, eventually, the family will totally depend. As a little boy, the first son goes to work with his father, to learn his trade. In later years he will provide for not only his parents but also for any widowed or unmarried women in his extended family. Eventually, he will even be the one to arrange for the father's funeral, light the funeral pyre, and carry out the ceremonies that will influence the course of the father's afterlife.

With so much invested in this child, the relationship of an Indian father and son is vastly different from its Western counterpart. The father finds it difficult to punish him, since the son is, in a sense, the keeper of his soul.

Damayanti tended to her two small children, and the small family thrived in their little two-room house, surrounded by dense groves of coconut palms. Life in the village was comfortingly routine. Sugunanandan was now simply referred to as Acchan, which means "father" in Malayalam. He and Damayanti rose at dawn to the sounds of birds and sacred chants echoing from the nearby Hindu temple. Acchan and most of the other village men mended their nets or headed out to sea to fish in their long, narrow wooden fishing boats. Any idle fishermen would usually go to the village tea stall to gossip over a cup of hot chai—a drink made with black tea, sugar, and boiled milk.

Typically the women of the village began their day by getting their older children ready for school. Although Kerala is a poor state, the government funds the children's schooling, and the literacy rate is almost 100 percent.

Damayanti usually spent the day helping with her husband's fishing business, cooking, washing the family's clothing, or, occasionally, crossing the backwaters on the ferry to shop for food and supplies in the village of Vallickavu. In addition to his house, Acchan built a small palm-thatched hut on the beach where the family would sometimes spend the night—lulled to sleep by the soothing sound of the ocean waves that lapped nearby.

Damayanti became pregnant with a third child, but the delivery did not go well and tragically, the baby did not survive the birth. Damayanti soon recovered and resumed her daily devotions, her housework, and tending to her two small children. During these years Acchan worked hard to expand his fishing business.

The monsoon rains would come to Kerala every June. In the parched heat of summer, where each breath felt to the villagers like breathing the air of an oven, suddenly a cool wind would begin to blow, and dark clouds would appear on the horizon. Insects, sensing the change in the air, would emerge from the parched earth, and man and beast would both pause in relief to savor the cool torrential rains that would begin to fall.

During the monsoon season in 1953, Damayanti began to have strange and vivid dreams of Hindu gods and goddesses. In recalling that time, Damayanti remembers vividly the dream in which she was visited by Lord Krishna—a form of God she had worshipped devotedly since she was a child. The energy of the dream was potent. Krishna regally stood before her, wearing gold silk robes and a golden crown decked with precious jewels and peacock feathers. His radiant blue face smiled tenderly at Damayanti, affecting her greatly with feelings of profound love and peace.

Although deeply moved by this dream, she mentioned it to no one, not even her husband, for there is a belief that it is not good to disclose such dreams to anyone. But although she remained silent about them, the dreams continued. Another night Damayanti had a dream of the Goddess Kali, who appeared to her wearing a blue and red silk sari with exquisite gold-thread embroidery. Kali's lips were bright red, and she wore a gold crown and held a sword in one hand and a trident in the other. Her smiling blue-black face and penetrating dark eyes radiated compassion and love.

In Hindu sacred art, Lord Krishna and the Goddess Kali are

Baby Krishna
(Courtesy of Amritapuri Ashram.)

portrayed as having blue or blue-black skin to symbolize the energy of enlightenment.

During the months of these vivid dreams, Damayanti discovered she was pregnant, but she had no idea when the baby would be due. She also found this child more difficult to carry than the previous three and worried that the baby might be in a bad position for the birth.

Finally, Damayanti had a dream that affected her so deeply, she could no longer keep quiet about it. She dreamed that she had given birth to the baby Lord Krishna and that she held Him tenderly in her lap while he suckled at her breast. She awoke feeling the dream meant good fortune and blessings for her family.

The next morning, while she and Acchan prepared the nets for fishing, she told her husband about the dreams she had been having. To her surprise, he was a little envious.

"You have so much time to give to prayer!" he told her. "That's why you have these dreams! I am too busy working to spend enough time in spiritual practice. That's why I haven't had such dreams."

Acchan recalls that not two weeks after this conversation with his wife he was visited in a dream by a huge golden cobra with its hood spread like a giant umbrella, under which stood Vishnu, the Lord of the Universe. Lord Vishnu was dressed in gold silk robes, and in his hands he held a conch shell, a discus, and a lotus blossom. As Acchan looked at Vishnu, he saw that all the thousands of Hindu gods and goddesses were merged as one within Him. All of divinity radiated from His form. As Acchan experienced this powerful vision, he was overcome with feelings of peace and divine blessing.

The next morning Acchan immediately told his wife of his dream.

"It was not a dream. I was wide awake, living the experience!" he told Damayanti. "I feel that an extraordinary gift has been given to me."

Now that they had both experienced these divine visitations, the couple could only laugh in astonishment. They both continued to have these dreams for the remainder of Damayanti's pregnancy.

It was the morning of September 27. Damayanti was on the beach, untangling a fishing net, when she suddenly had the sensation that she was going to go into labor. But since her body had not swelled the way it always did when she was going to give birth, she ignored the feeling and kept working. But the feeling persisted, and finally Damayanti put down the nets and walked,

Lord Vishnu
(Courtesy of Amritapuri Ashram.)
*It may appear to a Westerner that Hindus worship many gods, but in
fact, the various forms of the gods or goddesses represent different qualities of the One Absolute Consiousness that Westerners call God or
that Buddhists call the Clear Light of Consciousness.*

*According to Hindu tradition, whenever cosmic laws are broken and
chaos and evil threaten the world, Vishnu incarnates as an avatar to
fight the forces of disorder and to reestablish and maintain the sacred,
ethical, and moral order of dharma. Three of the most popular of
Vishnu's incarnations are said to have been Rama, Lord Buddha, and
Lord Krishna.*

by herself, back inland to the Idamannel home. She was gathering some things to take with her to her parents' house when she suddenly realized that the baby was on its way. She barely had time to spread a mat and lie down before the baby arrived.

Amma's entire birth, on September 27, 1953, was silent, and Damayanti said she felt almost nothing. When she looked at her newborn girl, Damayanti was shocked to see that her skin was dark blue. Remembering her last baby, who had not survived the birth, Damayanti was horrified, assuming that since this baby was silent and blue, that it was also dead. Damayanti began to cry. At that moment, a woman from a neighboring house happened to stop at the open door of the Idamannel house. Quickly realizing that Damayanti had just delivered a child, she hurried to make mother and baby comfortable. After assuring the shaken mother that the baby was alive and breathing, Damayanti again looked at the baby's face and was amazed to see the baby's dark eyes looking directly into hers. The baby looked back at her with a penetrating gaze and a benevolent smile on her tiny face.

Damayanti, however, was still not convinced that her child was all right. The child's legs were locked in a cross-legged position, like the lotus posture used for meditation. Her little thumbs and forefingers touched, each tiny hand forming a circle. Neither woman noticed how similar the baby's hand gestures were to the finger position yogis use to represent the ego merging with the Higher Self. Instead, they both thought she had some kind of skin and bone disease. Babies had been born in the village with twisted, deformed bones before and needed splints to straighten them out.

When Acchan arrived, both mother and father looked at the baby with grave concern. The silent, smiling baby did not look like a healthy newborn. When a doctor arrived at the house, he took one look at the baby's blue skin and said, "No baths for six months." He did not attribute her skin color to heredity, since both parents were light tan in skin tone. It turned out that this same doctor had seen a discolored baby born previously in the village, who had been given a bath by his parents soon after birth. But that baby died a few days later. So Amma was simply wrapped in a cloth, unbathed. Over the next few weeks, her crossed legs straightened out by themselves, and over time, her dark blue skin turned to dark brown.

Amma's parents gave her the name Sudhamani (Ambrosial Jewel).

Damayanti tried her best to settle into life with two small children and this strangely colored infant. It never occurred to her that this newborn infant might have anything at all to do with her dreams.

There was no celebrating, no heralding Sudhamani's birth with feasts, no prayers of gratitude said by Acchan at the temple, as had been done at Subhagan's birth.

Girls were not considered equal to boys and were often made to work longer and harder. In Kerala's remote villages, a girl's marital dowry could often be a great burden to a poor family. In Sudhamani's case, she was the second daughter and had very dark brown skin in comparison to the rest of her relatives and family. Hundreds of years ago, a prejudice toward fair-skinned people had infiltrated Indian consciousness as a result of foreign invaders. This dark child, then, seemed predestined to live a life of hardship and misunderstanding.

From the time she was an infant, Sudhamani was given no love and was treated poorly and impatiently by her parents and siblings.

Recalling the early years of ill treatment by her family, Amma said, "From all those experiences I clearly understood that the world is full of sorrow. We have no true relations, for all our relatives love us only to fulfill their own selfish needs. Human beings love each other out of desire. Nobody loves us selflessly. Only God loves us with selfless love."

.   .   .

Many years before Sudhamani's birth, Mahatma Gandhi had fought against the influence of foreign rulers on Hindu society. He also quite sternly criticized the bigotry of the Hindu caste system and Indian's passion for male progeny.

Kerala was particularly entrenched in the caste system, which formally ranked and segregated people according to the role they played in society as priests, warriors, merchants, and laborers. Gandhi went to Kerala in 1924 to join a massive protest against a practice that kept lower castes from using roads near certain temples. A person born into the lowest laborer caste was not allowed to eat or mingle freely with Brahmins, who were viewed as superior.

Although the belief in male supremacy dominated India, Gandhi's conviction was that women were intellectually, mentally, and spiritually equal to men. Not denying his own prejudice, he related in his autobiography how he too had wanted to dominate his wife in the early years of their marriage. He often said that the paternalistic society was the root cause of inequality, and that as long as people did not consider girls to be equal to boys, India as a nation would be in a dark eclipse.

Chapter 2

A DARK ECLIPSE

A LIFE OF SUFFERING AND PREJUDICE *(1953–1969)*

India was not the only country to experience a dark eclipse. At the time of Sudhamani's birth and early life, a dark cloud of human suffering enveloped the earth. Women everywhere were mistreated, and "informal castes" based on religion, gender, race, skin color, and wealth existed in every country.

Many concerned spiritual and political leaders supported legislation to stem the inequities and human atrocities. However, deeply ingrained cultural prejudice is not so easily legislated out of the human psyche. In 1947, great social and political changes had taken place in India with the achievement of independence from the British Empire. Many Indians fought hard for political, economic, and social reforms, and over the decades these reforms have taken root—except in the poor, remote villages of India.

These reforms were similar to those in the United States to free the black slaves in the 1800s, or to give women the right to vote in 1920. After all, Martin Luther King Jr. in the 1950s still had to fight for black civil rights in the South, and women in 1963 still had to inaugurate a women's rights movement.

On June 5, 2000, U.N. Secretary General Kofi Annan at the opening of the special General Assembly declared that "much remains to be done" to achieve equality for women. He expressed hope that the conference would "put the world on notice that not only do women belong on this planet, but that the future of this planet depends on women." He cited the increasing violence against women despite legislation and "a worldwide plague" of trafficking of women and children.

And so, in the poor, remote village where Sudhamani grew up, old cultural conditioning still ruled the fisherfolks' interaction with one another.

One day, when Sudhamani was five months old, Damayanti left the house, leaving the baby in the care of Acchan. Sudhamani began to cry. Acchan tried to quiet her, but Sudhamani continued to cry and wail. Finally, losing his patience, Acchan flung the baby onto a nearby cot.

Many years later, Sudhamani remarked to her father, "You know, the way you threw me that day, I thought you were trying to kill me!" It took a few moments before the astonished Acchan realized what she was referring to. Incredibly, she had remembered the incident.

Her ability to recall events from the time she was a baby was not the only way Sudhamani was unusual. Normal development of a female infant generally occurs as follows: sitting up at six months, crawling at nine months, beginning to walk at a year old, and beginning to speak in an articulate manner at about two and a half years.

The family was astonished, therefore, when one day shortly after turning six months old, Sudhamani simply stood up and walked across the veranda, thereby bypassing the normal developmental stages of crawling and toddling. Perhaps even more remarkable, soon afterward she began to speak Malayalam, her native tongue, fluently.

By the time she was two, Sudhamani had started to spontaneously pray and offer short songs in praise of Krishna. Overhearing her, the parents were taken aback. They had not taught Sudhamani these prayers and songs and had no idea how she knew them. Children of the village were magnetically attracted to Sudhamani. She loved to build miniature temples with them out of the muddy sand from the backwaters. She could be found talking very animatedly and lovingly to the trees, flowers, and animals around her. She had a pet green parrot that, if Sudhamani

Amma and parrot, San Ramon Ashram, California, 1996
When there is no mind or ego, then you are one with the whole of existence, and the universe with all its beings are your friends. —Amma

failed to give it enough attention, would tweak her nose. This always made the other children laugh.

Soon Damayanti became pregnant again. And although poor, Acchan managed to build another room alongside their cow shed.

But as the family grew, so too grew Sudhamani's religious fervor. By the age of five she was praying to Krishna and crying ardently for him almost unceasingly. She was often seen with tears streaming down her face—tears of yearning for Krishna. Her family was alarmed by this excessively emotional behavior.

Often, Sudhamani went into the woods, to sit alone and meditate. Or, during normal childhood play, she might suddenly stop and become withdrawn and meditative. Her parents would scold her for not being playful. They wanted her to fit in with the other children in the village. The family was also disturbed by her constant singing and chanting, and it bothered them that her lips were constantly moving, as if she were talking to herself. This was odd behavior for a small child, and they feared she had some mental illness.

The family did not understand that Sudhamani's lips were moving in silent prayers. "From birth itself I had an intense love of the Divine Name," she later said. "So much so, I would repeat the Lord's Name incessantly with every breath, and a constant flow of divine thoughts was kept in my mind irrespective of the place where I was or the work I was attending to."

When Sudhamani would take her younger siblings out to gather grass for the cows, they would see her "talking to herself" and, with the cruelty of children, begin to tease and belittle her for being weird. When they returned home they would tell their parents about her strange behavior, and Sudhamani would be beaten. Her parents were determined to make her a normal child, and they believed this could be achieved through harsh discipline. With a remarkable ability to forgive, however, Sudhamani continued to treat her siblings with kindness.

At the age of five, Sudhamani entered the Sraikkad School in a nearby village. She exhibited a remarkable intellect and memory. She had absolute retention—upon hearing a lesson once, she could recite it verbatim. By the time she was in second grade, she was first in her class, despite the fact that she was often absent in order to do household chores.

Her older brother and sister did not do so well. They were often scolded by the teachers for not doing their lessons properly. It did not make it easier for them that their oddly behaved younger sister was able to do these same lessons with utter ease. Because she was able to do her lessons so easily, she was able to do her homework during free moments during the school day. Then, when she returned home and had done her household chores, she was able to spend her remaining time in prayer.

By the time Sudhamani was nine years old, her mother, Damayanti, had given birth thirteen times. Of these thirteen children, only eight survived. Sudhamani's older brother and sister were away at college, and Sudhamani was now the eldest child at home. So many pregnancies and so much physical labor over her lifetime had weakened Damayanti's health, and by the time Sudhamani was in the fourth grade, Damayanti's health had completely deteriorated. She relied on Sudhamani more and more to do the household work that she could not do.

Because of Sudhamani's dark skin, and her strange, unchildlike behavior, she was viewed by her parents as inferior to the other children. They decided she should leave school and do domestic work full-time. All pretense of a normal childhood was now completely gone, and Sudhamani was doing nothing but household chores—from dawn until late into the night. It was common for her mother to coldheartedly wake the exhausted child before dawn by throwing cold water on her and to scream insults at her.

Years later Amma would simply say, "Damayanti was not punishing me. She treated me poorly only because of her limited vision. All those trials led me along the correct path, so I have no hatred toward her."

A day of work for young Sudhamani was a day of ceaseless chores. She would start the day by walking to the backwaters where the pungent scent of decaying coconut filled the air. She would fish a few coconut husks out of the water, which she would then pound to break down the fiber to make rope.

Later, as the sun began to rise, she would walk back home and sweep the house and yard. She would take large, heavy water pots to the village tap, fill them, and haul them back to the house. She would cook rice, feed the other children breakfast, and get them ready for school. After they had gone, she would wash the family's laundry by hand on the washing stone.

As she worked, Sudhamani would constantly pray and chant the name of Lord Krishna. In the afternoon she would milk the cows. She always did this with great love and respect because they were the cherished animals of Krishna. After the other children returned home from school, she would begin to cook dinner.

The most destitute often visited the Idamannel house, and in the Hindu tradition of charity, Damayanti and Acchan would give them food, oil, and clothing. They would, however, put the items some distance away from the house for the destitute to pick up; since these people were considered "untouchable," Damayanti and Acchan did not want to have any actual contact with them. Sudhamani, on the other hand, treated such people like family. She would take them extra food, and sit and eat with them. One

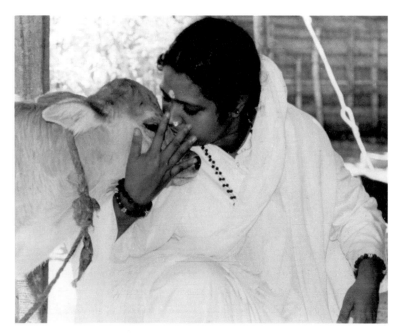

Amma and bliss-filled cow
(Courtesy of Amritapuri Ashram, 1995.)
Amma, who merged with Krishna's Consciousness, loves cows as much
as He did. Like many Hindus, she has always revered them as Divine
Mothers because they give so selflessly of themselves—not only their
milk, but also their skin and horns to be used for medicine and other
products after their death.

destitute man who visited regularly she respectfully called
"Accha" (father). Her parents were horrified to see her in contact with untouchables and forbade her to give away any more of
their food, but she continued to do so despite their punishments.

Her younger siblings, knowing Sudhamani's habit of giving
away food, would often pilfer food from the family's meager store-
room, knowing their older sister would be blamed for the loss and
punished instead of them. Sudhamani knew that they did this but
said nothing about it.

One day Sudhamani was out walking around the neighboring

houses, gathering vegetable scraps for the cows, when she met a starving family. Moved by their suffering, she returned home and took the one possession of value, a gold bangle belonging to her mother. Running back to the destitute family, she gave them the bangle so that they could sell it and buy food.

When Damayanti and Acchan returned home that evening and discovered that Damayanti's jewelry was missing, they both had a fit of uncontrolled fury at their daughter's rebelliousness. Acchan grabbed Sudhamani by the arm and dragged her outside, where he tied her to a tree. In a rage, he beat her with a palm frond until blood ran down her back.

Sudhamani spent that night in the family shrine in tears, praying and singing to Lord Krishna. "O my Beloved Krishna," she prayed, "nobody but You can understand my heart. This world is full of sorrow and suffering. People seek only their own happiness and pleasure. My darling Krishna I desire nothing else but complete oneness with You. O Lord, didn't You see my suffering today? O Lord, please come! These miseries are nothing for me, but the separation from You is agony."

The fishermen and their families from the coastal region of Kerala believed that fishing and its related tasks—sewing fishing nets and weaving rope out of coconut fiber—was the *only* work they were meant to do. They felt that any other type of work, such as domestic work, was beneath them. For this reason, it was hard to find domestic servants in that part of the country. The most common solution to this shortage was to force any young girl who was no longer attending school to take over the domestic duties of her family's household. It was also the custom to send such girls to the homes of relatives to work as domestic servants for them.

Such was the plight of young Sudhamani. Damayanti's mother persistently asked for Sudhamani's services, and when

Sudhamani was thirteen Damayanti and Acchan finally relented and sent her to various relatives to act as an indentured servant.

For the next three years, Sudhamani washed, cleaned, and cooked for their families, from whom she received no better treatment than she had from her own family. They too were alarmed and disturbed by her bizarre behavior and constant devotions, and tried to keep her from singing songs of praise as she worked. To them, she was just a dark-skinned, young domestic, a human being of almost no worth. Badly treated under the best of circumstances, she was cruelly beaten when caught giving away food to the destitute.

Finally, one day, after three years of backbreaking work, Sudhamani quarreled heatedly with her relatives.

"One day a situation will arise that you will have to come to me, begging for help," she told the astonished family. "Until that day comes, I will not set foot in this house again." With that, she left her relatives and returned to her family home in Parayakadavu.

But the situation Sudhamani returned to was, if anything, even worse than the one she had left. Damayanti was now suffering from rheumatoid arthritis, which had been aggravated by her having to resume household duties in Sudhamani's absence. This physical pain made her even more ill-tempered than she had been before.

One day her mother, who is still alive today, abused Sudhamani to the point of striking her with the handle of a machete used to open coconuts. Another time Damayanti cursed her, saying, "Let this defiant girl be damned! O God, why don't You put an end to her life?" When her parents took the other children to the temples for various religious festivals, they always left her behind.

Also, her relatives told her parents about the numerous times she had taken their food without asking, even though she did so to feed the poor. Thus Acchan and Damayanti felt that Sudhamani had brought shame and disgrace to the family name.

In addition, Subhagan, her elder brother, had returned from college and was now back at home with the family. While he was never the gentlest of souls, Subhagan had now become a true terror. He had a sadistic streak that he gratified by tormenting his younger siblings. When younger brother Satish made a mistake, Subhagan punished him by making him stand motionless for half an hour, bent over, with bricks on his back. Unfortunately, Subhagan was the eldest son, and therefore very little could be said against him. He had complete command over the rest of the family.

Because Subhagan was both an atheist and an extreme chauvinist, Sudhamani caught the full force of his anger. He believed that women should live the traditional Indian ideal—quiet, reserved, submissive, and obedient. The bizarre and deeply spiritual behavior of his sister ran contrary to everything he believed in.

When Sudhamani applied sacred ash between her eyebrows, in the place of her spiritual eye, Subhagan mocked her. "Are you becoming a monk?" he asked her. "Stop making such a show of yourself!"

When she received a checkered blouse as a gift, he snatched it out of her hands and set fire to it. "You're not modest enough!" he told her. "You're always trying to draw attention to yourself!" He again mocked her when she wore a silk jacket that she borrowed from one of her sisters. Finally, Sudhamani gave up trying to dress like other girls her age in the village. She decided she would only wear clothes given to her by the Lord—the old garments that other people had discarded.

Chapter 3

KRISHNA UNVEILED

A MIRACLE FOR THE SKEPTICS *(1970–1975)*

At age sixteen, Sudhamani was back in her own village and living with her family again. She continued to feel a strong desire to help other people. But with no money of her own, and with a life strictly controlled by her parents and older brother, she had virtually no means with which to do so. One day, however, she noticed that her neighbors were earning money by doing tailoring jobs, and she asked her parents if she could take a sewing class. They said no, but she continued to beg and plead until they finally agreed, on the condition that she complete her daily chores first.

Sudhamani began to take sewing classes in a parochial workshop in a Catholic chapel on the eastern shore of the backwaters. She took a half hour ferry ride across the backwaters to get to the chapel, which was located in a lovely open field. To the left of it was a small freshwater pond, to the right the Catholic cemetery. The pond was constantly visited by birds, and by cows that stopped to quench their thirst.

Sudhamani loved her sewing classes. Every day, she would hurry to get her chores done as soon as she could; then, dressed in a long skirt and a simple blouse, her hair pulled back in a ponytail, she would cross the backwaters on the ferry and happily take up her sewing.

While she sat sewing she would sing devotional songs, with tears of yearning for Krishna welling up in her eyes, while the other girls in the class giggled and gossiped among themselves. The elderly gray-haired priest who presided over the chapel noticed Sudhamani's pious devotion and became very fond of her.

Inside the chapel was an inner sanctum, where Sudhamani went to pray after she finished sewing. High on the wall was a crucifix, and gazing up at Jesus, Sudhamani decided that there was no difference between him and her beloved Krishna. The loving sacrifices made by both Jesus Christ and Krishna moved her deeply. "They sacrificed everything for the world! People turned against them, but they still loved them. If they have done it, why can't I? There is nothing new in it," she told herself.

Much as she loved the sewing classes, she was at the same time intensifying her spiritual practices. Between the classes, with the journeys there and back, and her huge burden of household chores, Sudhamani did not have enough hours in the day. She was forced to give something up. And so, after three years she decided to cease her sewing classes in order to spend more time in prayer and meditation.

The priest who was so fond of Sudhamani was being transferred to a monastery. He sent some girls from the sewing class to go to Sudhamani's village and give her the message that she should come and see him so that he could say good-bye.

Sudhamani, accompanied by her younger brother Satish, went back to the chapel where she had spent so many afternoons. When the priest saw her again, he burst into tears.

"My daughter, I am leaving this job," he said to her. "I am going to become a monk." And he bid her a loving good-bye.

Christ
(Courtesy of Self-Realization Fellowship.)
In the West, particularly in the Christian tradition, it is taught that only Christ was divine. However, Hindus believe that Christ, Buddha, and Krishna are but a few examples of the many great souls throughout history who have manifested their divinity.

As Sudhamani and Satish were leaving, the priest said to Satish, "Mark my words. Your sister will be acknowledged as a great soul during her lifetime."

By the time Sudhamani had turned nineteen, the spirituality and devotion she experienced in childhood had continued to grow and deepen, and she now spent virtually all her waking hours focused on God. With reverential humility she proclaimed and honored all life as the embodiment of the Divine. She hugged trees and animals, and kissed plants and small children as a way of acknowledging the presence of Krishna within them. Sometimes she would call small children aside and encourage them to enact the stories of Krishna's life. Forgetting that the children were playacting she would then hug them with great devotion because she believed they *were* Krishna. The devotional way in which Sudhamani hugged the children sometimes frightened them because they were unaccustomed to being treated in such an emotional manner.

Her devotion to Lord Krishna continued to increase. She composed numerous songs of devotion for him, which she would sing constantly, day and night. Not unlike the Christian mystics who had vivid visions of Christ, she would see Krishna before her, and He would take her hands and dance with her. She spent much of every night dancing in ecstasy, as if with Krishna himself.

Her interiorized states of consciousness were becoming more and more noticeable to the people around her. She often lost all sense of time and place. Having gone into the bathroom to take a bath, she might be found there hours later, completely oblivious to her surroundings. Or, having been sent to find the animals that had strayed from the Idammanel property during the day, she might not come back for hours. The sibling sent to fetch her would inevitably find her half-submerged in the backwaters, totally unconscious. At other times she just sat in the sand and

Sudhamani in ecstasy singing praises to God
(Courtesy of Mark Johnson, 1980.)
*According to her devotees, Sudhamani's soul-stirring devotional singing
transports them to a divine state of consciousness. Since her youth she
has composed over two hundred original devotional songs. Her music is
played all over India and in many other parts of the world.*

cried, seemingly for no reason. Perhaps not surprisingly her family, and in fact the whole village, was now beginning to believe that she suffered from a serious mental illness.

What do you do with a young woman like this? Her parents had one answer: marry her off as quickly as possible.

In India it is just assumed that a young woman will marry. Before independence, girls used to get married very early, and after the untimely deaths of their husbands, they were shunned by society. They were expected to shave their heads and live in isolation. Since independence, the laws concerning a woman's ability to divorce and remarry had become much more liberal, but in poor, remote areas the cultural and social attitudes surrounding single, divorced, and widowed women have, for the most part, not changed all that much. However, in India's large cities many women can go to work in offices, educational institutions, and factories without fear or hesitation.

As was the custom, Damayanti and Acchan arranged for the chaperoned visit of potential husbands for Sudhamani. (An arranged marriage does not mean that the bride is *forced* to marry a man her parents choose, but that her family chooses a few from which she can then make a choice.) The first two meetings with potential mates at Acchan's home were disastrous—Sudhamani was stubbornly resistant. However, her parents were determined to see her married and tried a third time.

Fearing that Sudhamani's strange behavior would bring yet more shame upon the family, Damayanti begged Sudhamani before the visitor's arrival, "Please, don't give this family a bad reputation. Please act politely and respectfully toward your future husband."

When the young man arrived and sat quietly in the living room, waiting to meet Sudhamani, she was in the kitchen, pounding dried red chilies with a wooden pestle. Suddenly, to everyone's shocked horror, she ran into the room screaming, brandishing the pestle like a weapon at the young man. Terrified, he ran out of the house.

Acchan vividly recalls the incident. "I had decided to get her forcefully married to this boy, but when the boy came to see her, Sudhamani came out with a stick to hit him. I was just shocked and stood there with a gaping mouth. I could see her running after him saying she'd kill him. It was very painful for me."

Amma later commented, "I was quite determined that if my parents continued to force me to marry, I would leave home and seek out a secluded place to continue my devotional practices."

The humiliation of this episode was almost unbearable for Damayanti, who had three other unmarried daughters, whose reputations and chances of marriage were in danger of being tainted by their "deranged" sister. In disgust, Damayanti harshly kicked and hit Sudhamani. Then, at a complete loss, she and Acchan sought out a well-known astrologer for advice on what to do with their out-of-control daughter.

After consulting Sudhamani's horoscope, the astrologer, who was a stranger to the family, turned to the parents and said gravely, "This girl is a mahatma (great soul)! If a marriage has not yet been arranged for this girl, please do not do so. Otherwise, it will be a cause of great sorrow for you."

So Damayanti and Acchan returned home with heavy hearts, not knowing what to do with their crazy daughter. They didn't *really* believe that she was a mahatma, but they were superstitious people and did not dare to do what an astrologer had told them not to do. So all plans to marry off Sudhamani were, for the time being, dropped. For the next two years, until she was twenty-one, she continued working for her family and taking care of her siblings.

But when Sudhamani was twenty-one, her life was changed forever. Sudhamani had always loved to hear stories about Krishna.

When she would overhear someone recounting such a tale, she would stop what she was doing and listen intently, often falling into a very deep meditative state—remaining motionless long after the story had ended.

One hot afternoon in September 1975, Sudhamani and her younger brother Satish were returning home after they had been out gathering grass for the cows. Balancing a large bundle of grass on her head, Sudhamani passed the entrance gate to the courtyard of their close neighbor Sree Retnam and overheard the family reading aloud the story of Krishna's birth from the Srimad Bhagavatam, a great epic chronicling Krishna's life. Sudhamani came to an abrupt halt and dropped her bundle of grass. When the reading ended Sree Retnam's family began singing devotional songs.

Sudhamani stood motionless, listening intently to the singing. Suddenly, she ran into the courtyard, to where the devotees were singing. To the utter astonishment of Sree Retnam and her family, who were gathered there, Sudhamani's body started vibrating and her facial features suddenly transformed into those of Lord Krishna!

Sree Retnam, who is still alive, recalls this moment as if it happened yesterday. "Sudhamani's dark brown skin suddenly became a blue-black color like Krishna and her eyes became luminous." Sree Retnam, through animated gesticulations, demonstrated how Sudhamani's body vibrated, and the way her hands assumed the very same yogic finger positions (mudras) and bodily stance of Krishna as He is portrayed in classic Hindu art.

Stunned at the changes that came over Sudhamani, Sree Retnam and the neighbors were convinced beyond a doubt that Krishna Himself had come to bless them in the form of this simple young woman. A few left the courtyard and ran off into the village to tell the news of this divine visitation. Word spread quickly throughout the village, and soon a large crowd of fisherfolk had gathered at the neighbor's compound. Some in the crowd were believers, but most were skeptics.

By that time, Sudhamani had returned to her normal physical state, although she was still in a state of divine bliss. She had asked for water and was sprinkling it on people as holy water. The skeptics in the crowd, having been summoned to see a divine spectacle, became impatient.

"If you really are Krishna, show us a miracle!" they called to Sudhamani. "Otherwise, how can we believe you?"

"You have the Real Gem inside you," Sudhamani replied. "Why do you want to see an imitation?"

But the crowd was not deterred by this.

"Prove to us that you have manifested Krishna!" they insisted. "Show us a miracle!"

"I am not interested in making believers by showing miracles," Sudhamani told them. "I am here to help you find the real truth, and to find liberation of the Self [Soul] through the realization of your eternal nature. Miracles are only illusions. Besides, if I perform one miracle, you will only want more and more of them. I am here to remove desire, not create it!"

"No, we won't ask for more!" the skeptics promised. "Just show us one!"

Finally, with no other way to pacify the crowd, Sudhamani acquiesced.

"In order to instill faith in you, I will perform one miracle," she announced.

The crowd buzzed excitedly.

"Let those who doubt come back here to this very spot on the day of the next Srimad Bhagavatam discourse," she said. "And then never ask me to perform one again." Having received her promise, the crowd slowly dispersed.

News of the divine visitation and the promised miracle to be performed spread like wildfire to the surrounding villages. By the time the appointed hour on the day of the next Bhagavatam discourse had arrived, about a thousand people had journeyed to the little fishing village to see the spectacle.

The prayer room at Sree Retnam's house, which was where Sudhamani intended to perform the miracle, was very small—only about five feet by twelve. The room had two windows—one on the south wall and one on the west wall. Beneath the window on the west wall was a long, narrow ledge that held several oil lamps, an incense burner, a vase of flowers, and a small copper pitcher of water that was used in prayer rituals. Above the ledge hung pictures of Lord Krishna.

Of course, the room was far too small for the multitudes that had gathered. Skeptics jammed into the little room and jostled for positions on the open-beamed rafters, hoping to catch Sudhamani in black magic or sleight-of-hand tricks from their vantage points. Others crowded into the adjoining room, where Damayanti herself waited. Some sat on the branches of trees outside while others crammed into the compound, elbowing to get a glimpse of Sudhamani. Her younger brothers Satish and Suresh, who witnessed the episode, said they stood outside the south wall window, looking right into the prayer room.

Sudhamani arrived at the appointed hour, wearing a simple blouse and ankle-length skirt, and asked that the oil lamps and incense be lit. Then she began to pray deeply and sang devotional songs to Krishna. Her appearance once again changed to reveal the face of Krishna.

Sudhamani pointed to Sri Kantan, who lived in her village, a man she knew to be a skeptic, and said, "Take the copper pitcher on the ledge and empty it. Then bring it to me filled with fresh water."

Outside, in view of everyone, Sri Kantan emptied the small pitcher onto the ground and refilled it from a nearby pipe.

Back in the prayer room, Sudhamani blessed the pitcher of water, saying prayers over it like a temple priest. Then she told Sri Kantan to dip his fingers into the water.

His fingers came out of the pitcher covered with milk! The crowd murmured with astonishment at this sight.

She told Sri Kantan to once again dip his fingers into the pitcher. He did so, and this time his hand came up covered with pudding!

Satish, who personally knew Sri Kantan, remarked in a 1997 interview, "He didn't believe Amma at the time, but he does now."

There was more reaction from the crowd, who buzzed and craned for a closer look. Clearly, something was taking place that could not be explained. The water had turned to milk, and then to pudding before their very eyes. Neither Sudhamani nor the pitcher had been out of their sight; there was no rational explanation for what had happened.

The pudding that had appeared in the pitcher, and that Sudhamani was now offering as a blessing from God, was a favorite dessert of Lord Krishna, called *panchamritam*, made of bananas, milk, raisins, and sugar. Its delicious scent quickly filled the small room.

Sudhamani motioned to her mother, Damayanti, who had been watching from the adjoining room, to come forth and be served some of this miraculous pudding. Damayanti came forward slowly, amazed and speechless. A new thought crossed her mind that perhaps Krishna actually was inside this child of hers. Twenty years later Damayanti remarked in an interview, "Changing water into pudding couldn't be done by an ordinary person. After that [miracle] I saw her [Sudhamani] as God."

Awestruck by what they had seen, most of the people present believed they had indeed witnessed a miracle, and that they were in the presence of Lord Krishna. They crowded around for a taste of this remarkable pudding.

Kasturi, Amma's older sister, commented, "I never tasted anything like it. It [pudding] had such a sweet aroma. One man who wanted to test the miracle took some of it home. He came back and told us that even after several days, the pudding still tasted good."

People ran out from the compound to spread the word of what had happened, and more people continued to arrive. Over the next several hours, well into the early hours of the morning, people continued to come to see for themselves this simple miracle and to sample the *panchamritam*. Although almost a thousand people were served out of the quart-size pitcher that night, somehow it was never depleted.

The skeptics that still remained near Sree Retnam's house called the event a case of mass hypnotism. They, along with everyone else, were at a loss to explain how it was that the sweet scent of the pudding lingered on people's hands for several days.

Many of the people who witnessed the changing of water into pudding are still alive today, including Sree Retnam, who proudly displays the prayer room in her humble home where the miracle took place.

There are countless stories from the Hindu tradition telling of great yogi saints who have performed miracles similar to those of Christ. It is said that great yogis who are one with God, and who experientially understand that our physical reality is but an electronic dream world of God, can through the power of thought, visualization, and will command the elemental atoms to combine and manifest in any form they wish.

Many more people were drawn to visit Sudhamani after hearing about the miracle of the pudding. For the next six months, several times a week Sudhamani took on the same classical appearance of Lord Krishna (an occurrence she called Krishna Bhava) and blessed the people who came to see her. *Bhava* means "mood" or "quality of God." Each Hindu deity represents one or more of the infinite qualities of the One God or Absolute Consciousness. Sudhamani later commented about these divine

Sudhamani in Krishna Bhava
Before Sudhamani gave her darshan as Krishna, her devotees put a crown with peacock feathers on her head.

moods. "All the deities of the Hindu pantheon, who represent the infinite aspects of the one Supreme Being, exist within us as well. The divine mood of Krishna is the manifestation of the pure consciousness aspect of Absolute Consciousness."

Sudhamani chose a small banyan tree on the western seaside of Idamannel where she could dance, say her prayers, and give her blessings, or darshan. Although she performed no more public miracles, people reported that when they went to Sudhamani for her darshan (blessing) and unburdened their troubles to her, they were often miraculously healed of what had ailed them. News of these healings spread quickly. Soon people were coming to see Sudhamani not only from across Kerala, but from other parts of India too.

Sudhamani's father, Acchan, had been away on business on that first occasion of Krishna Bhava. When he came back and heard what had happened, he immediately assumed Sudhamani's unusual behavior was part of the mental disease he and his wife had feared she was suffering from.

However, he wanted to see for himself what was going on. So he arranged for another reading of the story of Krishna's life, as told in the Bhagavatam, to take place at his home. During the reading at his home, in front of his own eyes, Acchan saw his daughter's body vibrate, change color, and take on the traditional pose of Lord Krishna. It was unmistakable. For a man such as Acchan, who had been a devoted follower of Krishna all his life, it was an awe-inspiring sight. He became an ardent believer from that moment onward.

The stories that everyone was telling about the healings affected other members of the family too. Satish, one of Sudhamani's younger brothers, who had seen the miracle of the pudding, still found it difficult to believe that his strangely behaved older sister actually had divine qualities. But he was beginning to hear so many stories about her otherworldly powers that he began to wonder if they could possibly be true.

Satish had suffered with asthma until he was twelve years old. Although he had been hospitalized for the asthma, it had gotten worse rather than better. Years later Satish shared how he came to believe in his sister. He said, "In the beginning we [our family] didn't have faith in Amma. Personally, I wanted to test her. I asked her to cure my asthma during the Krishna Bhava."

He approached his sister, saying, "You know that I have asthma, and it is getting worse. Please cure my asthma, or I am going to die."

Sudhamani looked lovingly at Satish. She hugged him and rubbed sacred ash on his forehead.

Satish said, "Since then, I've never had asthma. Then I realized that she had some powers."

Sudhamani's family, and the village at large, now believed that she was possessed by Lord Krishna during the Krishna Bhava. Even so, once the darshan was over, Damayanti, amazingly, persisted in her abusive attitude. Sudhamani's mother, along with a number of villagers, mistakenly believed that when the darshan was over, Sudhamani returned to being a simple domestic servant. For her part, Sudhamani did not try to convince them of anything different.

Historically, in the West as well as in India, there are numerous examples of individuals whose bodies are temporarily possessed by God or spirits, while in ecstatic states of devotion, similar to those of the Apostles on Pentecost Sunday who spoke in tongues, transmitting the gifts of the Holy Spirit, or those of the Greek oracles of Delphi, who channeled the god Apollo. In this manner, Sudhamani's parents and the local villagers thought that her body was a temporary vehicle for Krishna to use.

Acchan himself had the Krishna Bhava darshan permanently moved from under the seaside banyan tree to Idamannel. During one darshan, Sudhamani called her father aside and predicted what was to happen in the future.

Acchan vividly recalls her words to him. "In time, this place will become a spiritual center. Many of my devotees will flock here from far and wide, and some will settle here. I myself will travel around the world, many times.

"You are going to suffer a lot in the near future. The villagers, and even your own relatives, are going to hate and abuse you. But do not be afraid. God will bless you and provide for your needs."

Acchan was astonished by her predictions. His little Sudhamani, the uneducated servant girl, was going to travel the world? And Idamannel, his humble home, was going to become a spiritual center? It did not seem possible.

He did not even want to think about her third prediction—that he would have to suffer a great deal in the future. It was such an unpleasant thought that he put it out of his mind. Only many years later would he acknowledge the utter truth of what she had predicted that day.

Chapter 4

THE DIVINE MOTHER AWAKENS

Assassination Attempts by Antagonists *(1976–1977)*

Although Sudhamani very quickly became widely known as word spread of her abilities to heal, not everyone was enamored of her. In fact there was one large group that was not happy about her practices at all.

According to Professor M. Ramakrishnan Nair, a man who lives in Amma's village, a thousand young "rationalists" joined together from thirteen coastal villages. They firmly believed that God would never show His divinity through a human form and resided *only* in the sacred icons in the sanctum sanctorum of the temples. They claimed that what Sudhamani was doing was false, as well as blasphemous, and they were determined to expose her as a charlatan. They formed a group they called the Committee to Remove Blind Beliefs, with the goal of putting an end to her darshans.

They started visiting Idamannel in groups, with the intention of seizing Sudhamani and roughing her up. They would arrive and stand for hours, watching Sudhamani blessing throngs of villagers, but somehow, oddly, once they were actually in her presence, they couldn't bring themselves to carry out their plan. Finally, they would leave.

According to Professor Nair, finding themselves unable to strike out against Sudhamani, the rationalists hired a black magician to do the job for them. The black magician, who was infamous for his deadly sorcery, prepared ash from the charred body of a cobra and chanted evil mantras over it. It would, he assured the group, prove fatal to anyone it was given to.

Twenty years later Acchan recalled that during one of the Krishna Bhavas, a man appeared at Idamannel, carrying a bowl of ash. Acchan thought the man was a monk because he was wearing ochre-colored robes and had ash smeared on his forehead. But Acchan said Sudhamani was not deceived.

"That man is a black magician," she whispered in her father's ear. "Please bring him to me."

Acchan by this time was aware that his daughter could read people's minds. He had personal experience of it because he said she had read his mind numerous times. Therefore he was not surprised that his daughter knew of the man's intentions to harm her. When Acchan brought the man over to her, the magician bowed in the traditional Indian manner and offered her the deadly ash. Fully aware of what he was giving her, Sudhamani took the ash and rubbed it over her body and face. "If I will perish from this, then let it be so," she said to herself. "It is God's will."

The black magician waited to see her collapse in agony, but she did not. Finally, under the coldhearted gaze of the rationalists who had come to witness Sudhamani's death, he shrank away in utter, humiliated defeat. Acchan recalls that a short time later he returned and begged Sudhamani for forgiveness.

Although Acchan is unable to remember the man's name, he says that the man, who lives quite a distance from the ashram, became a devotee and remains one to this day. He comes to the ashram at different times for Amma's blessing.

Rajappan and his wife lived in a small town called Sraikad, about ten kilometers from Sudhamani's village. They were rationalists and skeptics who put Sudhamani through another severe test. During one of the Krishna Bhavas, Rajappan and his wife entered the temple with a glass of milk, into which they had poured a strong poison. Graciously smiling, Sudhamani took the glass of milk, touched it to her forehead in acceptance, and then drank the whole glass. They waited anxiously for Sudhamani to go into convulsions. After a few moments Sudhamani turned in their direction, vomited the poisonous milk, then continued receiving devotees as if nothing had happened. Shocked that she survived, Rajappan and his wife left the temple. A short time later they became devotees and confessed to Acchan and his family that they had added poison to the milk.

Sudhamani was deeply moved by the people she met who were sad and suffering, and would spontaneously give them a tender, compassionate hug. When others saw this they too wanted to be comforted in the same way. So this became the maternal and natural way that Sudhamani blessed and loved everyone, regardless of their age, caste, sex, or religion.

In India, a virtuous woman (especially an unmarried woman) does not hug and indiscriminately associate with people, especially men. Sudhamani's manner of receiving devotees immediately caused talk in the village. Rumors were spreading that she was a disreputable woman.

Subhagan heard these rumors and was incensed. Once again, his sister was bringing shame and dishonor upon the family. He severely rebuked Sudhamani and forbade her to continue hugging people, a command that she completely ignored.

By this time Acchan had turned half his cowshed, which was attached to his home, into a little temple for his daughter to give her darshan. One day, in an attempt to prevent Sudhamani from holding darshan, Subhagan deliberately broke the oil lamp in the temple. When Sudhamani and her devotees found the broken lamp, the devotees were dismayed, but Sudhamani seemed unconcerned.

Sree Retnam, who lived next door to Acchan's home, witnessed what occurred next. She said that Sudhamani told her and the other people to go to the beach and gather some seashells. Since there was no more oil, she asked them to fill the shells with water and place oil wicks in them. She then asked them to light the wicks. Then the impossible happened: the wicks stayed lit and burned through the night.

When asked how this was possible, Sudhamani replied, "The lamps burned because of the faith of the devotees."

Subhagan, seeing that his sister had ignored his command to stop the Krishna Bhavas, decided to ban her from the house. When she returned one day from the temple and attempted to go into the family home, he stood at the doorway and blocked her entrance.

"You may not come into this house!" he told her. "Until you stop your shameful behavior of singing, dancing, and mixing freely with all kinds of people, you will not be permitted inside."

As a result, Sudhamani was forced to start living outside, sleeping on the damp earth under a palm tree.

Subhagan's abusive nature did not go unnoticed by the family. His parents in an interview years later said, "We were deeply concerned about his mental health, and even though we took him to several priests and doctors, he continued to be aggressive, violent, and bad tempered."

Satish said that one day, when Subhagan was spurned by a young woman in the village, he went into a vile mood. Turning his anger on Sudhamani, he and his cousin, Satyasilan, called her to a relative's house on a false pretext. When she arrived, they surrounded her and Satyasilan threatened her with a large knife.

"Your behavior has gone too far!" Subhagan told her. "Since you can't stop bringing shame upon the family, it is better that you be dead!"

Sudhamani's tranquil reply infuriated him.

"I am not afraid of death," his sister told him calmly. "The body must meet its end sooner or later, but it is impossible for you to kill the Self. But I have a last wish, which you are obliged to fulfill. Let me meditate for a while, and then you can kill me while I am in meditation."

"Who are you to command us?" Satyasilan, her cousin, growled. "Are we here to kill you or not kill you according to your wish?"

Sudhamani smiled. "Nobody but God can put an end to my life."

As if to prove her wrong, Satyasilan jumped forward and tried to stab her in the chest. But at the very moment the tip of the knife made contact with her body, he felt an excruciating pain in the very same place in his own chest. Agonized, he dropped the knife, clutched his chest, and fell to the floor.

At that moment, Damayanti was approaching the house. Hearing the cousin's screams of pain, she ran inside. Immediately seeing that her daughter was trapped with these violent young men, she grabbed Sudhamani by the hand and rushed her away.

According to Amma's father, Satyasilan was taken to Sankar's Hospital in Quilon, where doctors were at a loss to explain his condition. Acchan and Sudhamani went together to visit him in the hospital. Sudhamani sat at his bedside and comforted and fed him with her own hands. Acchan said that Satyasilan wept, so moved was he by her compassion.

Despite the excellent medical care he received in the hospital, Satyasilan's health continued to deteriorate, and he died a few days later, vomiting blood.

One day, in March 1977, Sudhamani was sitting alone inside the family home, meditating. Her eyes were open, but she was in a deeply introspective state. Suddenly, a globe of brilliant light appeared before her, as red as the setting sun. Against the backdrop of this orb of light emerged the enchanting form of the Goddess with a beautiful crown on her head.

Sudhamani was so moved by this beautiful sight that she cried out. When the vision faded, Sudhamani called to Krishna.

"O Krishna, Mother came! Please take me to Her, I want to embrace Her!"

Sudhamani felt herself being lifted by Krishna up to the clouds. There she saw strange visions—steep hills, blue snakes, and vast, dense forests. But no Divine Mother.

From that moment on, Sudhamani wanted only to again see the lovely, smiling face of the Divine Mother. Until that time, Sudhamani had only worshipped Krishna, whom she thought to be the highest divinity. Seared by this exquisite vision, Sudhamani now dedicated herself completely to a search for the Divine Mother.

In the past, although deeply spiritual, Sudhamani had always bathed and dressed herself and efficiently performed all her daily chores. Now, however, she completely abandoned herself to the world of the divine and stopped taking proper care of herself. She stopped eating and bathing. Her parents, and the people of the village, believed she had completely succumbed to her mental illness.

Luckily, she received the compassionate care of a few of the village women. "Poor girl!" they remarked. "Her parents have just abandoned her. When she was healthy, she cooked and cleaned for them, but now that she is unwell, they have discarded her." So these women bathed, dressed, and fed Sudhamani during this period of heightened austerity and spiritual transformation.

During this time, Sudhamani was extremely sensitive to food. The only food she could eat was food prepared while the holy name of God was chanted. However, she could drink the milk from cows and eat the food that an eagle brought her. Her mother, Damayanti, witnessed how an eagle would circle overhead above

Sudhamani and drop a fresh fish into her lap. Sudhamani, most of the time, ate the fish raw. But Damayanti said that a few times she grabbed the fish out of her daughter's lap and cooked it for her.

While Sudhamani's most profound spiritual transformation was taking place, she often suffered extremes of heat. At those times she had to cool her body in the damp sands of the beach or in the backwaters, where she would stand meditating with the water up to her chin. Her body felt as if it were burning, as if it had been rubbed with hot chilies.

Although she went through extreme physical and emotional agonies, at the end of this period Sudhamani went into samadhi—a state of deep meditation in which she felt extreme bliss and happi-

Sudhamani merges with the Divine Mother
(Courtesy of Amritapuri Ashram.)

ness. She experienced the Divine Mother merging within her as a living form brilliantly illuminated and dazzling as a thousand suns. Sudhamani tried to make this mystical union intelligible through the following composition she wrote, titled "The Path of Bliss":

> *Once upon a time, my soul was dancing in delight through the path of bliss. At that time, all the inner foes such as attraction and aversion ran away, hiding themselves in the innermost recesses of my mind.*

> *Forgetting myself, I merged in a golden dream which arose within me. As noble aspirations clearly manifested themselves in my mind, the Divine Mother, with bright, gentle hands, caressed my head. With bowed head, I told Mother that my life is dedicated to Her.*

> *Smiling, She became a divine brilliance and merged in me. My mind blossomed, bathed in the many-hued Light of Divinity and the events of millions of years gone by rose up within me. Thenceforth, seeing nothing as separate from my own Self a single Unity, and merging in the Divine Mother, I renounced all sense of enjoyment.*

> *Mother told me to ask the people to fulfill their human birth. Therefore, I proclaim to the whole world the sublime Truth that she uttered, "Oh mind, merge in your Self!"*

> *Thousands and thousands of yogis have taken birth in India and lived the principles visualized by the great sages of the unknown past. To remove the sorrow of humanity, how many naked truths there are!*

> *Today I tremble with bliss recollecting Mother's words, "Oh my darling, come to Me, leaving all other works. You are always Mine."*

Before her transformation, Sudhamani had perceived everything to be pervaded by Krishna. Now, however, she saw the limitless divinity of the feminine aspect of God reflected in everything—the countless stars in the night sky, the radiant sun, the earth and all its life-forms. She perceived that the universe itself was Divine Mother's physical body.

Years later Sudhamani said, "There are six chakras, or centers of spiritual power in the human body. The vital life force [Kundalini Shakti] that flows through all living beings is called serpent power, and it rests below the base of the spine in the form of a coiled, sleeping female snake.

Symbolic drawing of the chakras
(Courtesy of the author.)

"When this power is awakened, through incessant meditation, it ascends through the spine, passing through the chakras. When each chakra is reached, the physical body can suddenly become very hot, and the person may start to sweat profusely. He or she may also have visions, both divine and earthly. When the serpent power has transcended all six chakras, it rises to the top of the head—to the crown chakra. At that moment the body suddenly experiences a refreshing coolness as it is transformed into a new vessel of tremendous spiritual power."

Spiritual transformation is part of awakening to who we are. It happens to Christian mystics as well as to Hindus, as the life of the Christian monk Padre Pio demonstrates. Padre Pio (1887–1968) experienced the wounds of Christ in his body, known as stigmata. An article, available from the Padre Pio Foundation of America, states that when Padre Pio was a young monk he experienced extreme heat in his body—so much so that the doctor taking his temperature had to use a horse thermometer because normal thermometers would shoot the mercury right through the top.

Padre Pio was always immersed in repeating the holy names of God, but from his Christian tradition. He had great devotion to Christ and an incessant love of the Blessed Virgin Mary. Many miracles were ascribed to him, and he was known to read minds, eat little, and barely sleep but two hours a night.

Like Sudhamani, Padre Pio experienced a period of persecution by the poor villagers he grew up with and with the Vatican hierarchy before his sanctity was recognized.

In Sudhamani's village there was virtually no electricity and no television, cars, radios, phones, or movie houses to distract people's attention. Everyone knew everyone else's business, as happens in remote villages even today. Thus, Sudhamani's strange behavior and purported healing gifts caused her to become the major focus of attention and the subject of village gossip.

In contrast, New York City and other large metropolitan areas have a lot of distractions that tend to keep people cynically insular. In July 1998 when Amma was in New York City, the *Village Voice* ran an article that read, "Can a person be forgiven for thinking that, if someone came running to say he'd just seen Jesus preaching on the steps of the 72nd Street subway stop, most New Yorkers would reply, 'Whatever'? This is a tough market for prophets. It's not an easy town for seekers, either, which may be why so many of those who've come to Central Park West to see the woman they call 'Ma' appear to be from elsewhere."

That Sudhamani was so severly tested by the rationalists and villagers would not seem unusal to Indians. Dr. Jim Ryan, an expert in Asian religious traditions and present cochair of Asian and Comparative Studies at the California Institute of Integral Studies said, "Saints in India, those that are generally accepted by Indians, are submitted to an acid test far more intense than they might be given by gullible Western followers. There is a rich Indian folklore known in the villages about the false holy man and those claiming to be enlightened who are subjected to intense scrutiny.

"Even the great Ramakrishna Paramahansa, arguably one of the greatest saints India has seen in the last few centuries, was suspected of being a madman rather than a mystic. He would go off into long trances where he would commune with the Divine Mother Kali. A great many people in Calcutta judged him to be crazy. It was only when he had been closely examined personally by two highly respected pundits [authorities on Hindu scriptures] and had been declared by them to be authentic that he began to receive wider acceptance."

Dr. Ryan said the fact that Amma is now so revered in India

Ramakrishna Paramahansa, 1836–1886

Today many Indians from North India believe that Amma is a reincarnation of Ramakrishna or of his saintly wife Sarada Devi. Amma greatly respects this great saint.

Ramakrishna, a poor Bengali Brahmin priest, became a devotee of the goddess Kali and lived at her temple in Dakshineswar outside Calcutta. He experienced union with God by practicing the religious disciplines from various traditions including Christianity and Islam.

He then taught that all religions were a valid means of knowing God and attaining enlightenment.

means she has passed very severe scrutiny and therefore she has been accepted by a great number of Indians as a genuine mystic.

Sudhamani's parents were used to hearing her make predictions about future events. In recalling this earlier period, Acchan said at first they did not believe her and so mostly they forgot or ignored what she told them. However, one day in 1977, Sudhamani and her mother were traveling when Sudhamani turned

Sudhamani and her mother Damayanti
(Courtesy of Mark Johnson, 1980.)

to Damayanti and said calmly, "You know, I believe that Subhagan does not have much longer to live—maybe a year. It is just a feeling I have, so I am telling you."

Damayanti was deeply distressed to hear such a dire prediction about the fate of her eldest son. "Is there anything I can do?" she asked.

"You can take a vow of silence," Sudhamani told her. "But situations will arise to try to make you break your vow, and if you do so, you will make matters even worse for him. So you must be very, very careful if you decide to take the vow."

When they returned home and Damayanti told Acchan what Sudhamani had predicted, he too was deeply upset.

After considering her daughter's words, Damayanti decided to take a vow of silence for one day. But during that day, in the afternoon, she was out in the yard when she saw one of the cows break its rope and bolt from the cowshed.

"A cow has broken loose!" she yelled out before she realized what she had done.

The family took this as a very bad omen, and the belief that Damayanti had made Subhagan's situation worse threw the family into a state of fear and dread.

Chapter 5

CALL TO COMFORT
THE SUFFERING
A PERIOD OF CHAOS *(1977–1979)*

One day in 1977, not long after her mystical union with the Divine
Mother, Sudhamani sat absorbed in meditation on the edge of the
Arabian Sea, which was aglow with the dusky reflections of a fuch-
sia-streaked sky. While meditating, she heard from within her the
voice of the Divine Mother: "My child, I am present everywhere
and dwell in the hearts of all beings. Your life is not for merely enjoy-
ing the pure bliss of your individual soul, but for comforting suffering humanity. Henceforth, honor my presence in the hearts of all
beings, and relieve them of the sufferings of worldly existence."

From that moment on, Sudhamani began manifesting the
qualities of the Divine Mother as well as Krishna. The devotees
who wished to see Sudhamani adorned with a silk sari and a
crown during the Devi Bhava, offered her these items as gifts and
pleaded for her to accept them. Out of respect, over the next couple of years (1977–1978), the devotees began calling her Amma,
which means "Mother" in the Malayalam language.

The experience of hearing the voice of God/Goddess within has
been a common experience for mystics across cultures. Christian
mystic Saint Hildegard of Bingen many times heard within her the

voice of God, who she said gave to her many revelations, which she dutifully recorded. Mystics from various traditions have testified that God, or Absolute Consciousness, is the very nature of our being, and that it can be experienced as a very real living presence within us.

The Tibetan Buddhist monk Lama Yeshe said, "Tantra challenges this unreasonably low opinion of human potential by showing us how to view ourselves and all others as transcendentally beautiful—as gods and goddesses in fact." Jesus Christ challenged the Pharisees in a similar way when he said, "Is it not written in your law. 'I said Ye are gods?' "

Each of Sudhamani's manifestations revealed a different quality of divinity. In the mood of Krishna (Krishna Bhava), she said she felt no sense of either compassion or lack of compassion for anyone. She experienced a meditative aloofness from people's suffering.

However, in the mood of the Divine Mother, she felt nothing but love and compassion for every living being. During the Devi Bhavas she held devotees tenderly in her arms and whispered in their ears, "Darling, darling son," or "Darling, darling daughter." Listening attentively to their sorrow-filled stories, she alleviated some of their suffering.

Several years later, much to the disappointment of her Krishna devotees, Sudhamani made a conscious decision to permanently manifest *only* love and compassion, qualities Hindus attribute to the Divine Mother, or feminine aspect of God. She said, "I felt this was what our world needed."

When she began to manifest the qualities of the Divine Mother, her facial expressions and temperament changed. Along with being gentle and all-forgiving, she now could become angry and disciplinary when seeing someone wronged. Instead of patiently suffering cruelty from her brother and parents, she stood up to them and challenged their abusiveness.

Amma's utter fearlessness was demonstrated one day in the temple. Her paternal grandmother, Srimati Mahavi (Achamma), tells the story of how she and the villagers were afraid of the cobras that flourished in Kerala's tropical habitat. Such cobras are so poisonous that one bite can render a fully grown man unconscious within minutes, and dead soon after that, with no time to administer an antidote. Achamma said, "For several weeks, a large cobra had been seen in the village and provoked so much terror that I and other people stopped walking at night on the seashore path."

By this time Achamma, having witnessed the numerous practical things that Amma had done to help the villagers, went to ask her advice on what should be done about the snake. Amma simply replied that the snake would not hurt her.

"But one day, soon after," Achamma said, "when Amma was giving darshan, the snake suddenly slithered into the temple. It approached Amma, its hood spread and its tongue was flicking like it was prepared to strike. We screamed in fear and scattered to get away from the snake. Then Amma stuck out her tongue, grabbed the snake, and touched its flicking tongue to her own! As she put it down she told the snake, 'This is my grandmother. Don't hurt her.' "

The snake immediately left the temple and was never seen again.

Around this same time period, Amma's experiences changed in a profound way. In the past, her meditations had been focused on God in the various, personal physical forms (such as in the forms of Divine Mother, Krishna, or Lord Siva). She found that whatever form of God she meditated on, she became totally merged with the peculiarities of that form. Similar experiences occurred in the Western world for Saint Francis, Padre Pio of Italy, and Theresa Neumann of Germany, who so deeply meditated on the suffering of Christ that they manifested the crucifixion wounds (stigmata) of Christ in their bodies.

One day while meditating, Amma said she experienced God as the primal sound of Aum, the formless reality beyond all attributes of a particular form of God.

The great sages of India taught that the whole world is a creation from the sacred sound of Aum, called nada Brahma. The Vedic tradition teaches that "Aum" is the *feminine creative principle*—the formless Goddess—the sacred sound and vibration of Consciousness, which sustains, destroys, and creates all physical forms in the universe. Sufi master Hazrat Khan said, "This sound is the source of all manifestation. The knower of the mystery of sound knows the mystery of the whole universe." Physicists call this primal sound the "Big Bang."

Years later Amma tried to put this profound mystical experience into words:

"One day, when meditating, I heard a terrific humming sound and perceived the form of Devi [Divine Mother]. Suddenly I realized that I myself am Devi and that the humming sound also was being produced by me. I thought 'What is this? How have I become Devi? Maybe this is a trick played by the Divine Mother to obstruct my spiritual practice.' So I thought, 'Let me meditate on Lord Siva and see what happens,' but the moment I began meditating on Lord Siva's form, I became Him. I thought, 'Maybe Siva is also testing me.' So I stopped meditating on his form.

"Whichever form of god or goddess I contemplated, I became. Then I heard a voice from within, 'You are not different from them. Both God with attributes and the formless God are within you. Seek to realize your oneness with the formless aspect.' Then I started chanting 'Aum' and directly experienced that everything is Brahman, the Absolute.

"From that day onward I could see nothing as different from my own formless Self, wherein the entire universe exists as a tiny bubble."

Amma's mystical experience is known in the Vedantic tradition as nondual awareness. Such awareness happens when the meditator and that which is meditated upon merge into one formless unified field of Absolute Consciousness. Saint Teresa of Avila also experienced the formless aspect from the Christian tradition when she testified, "I have seen the formless Christ."

The Hindus have two spiritual symbols that signify that aspect of God as the primal sound of Aum—the Sanskrit symbol for Aum and the Sri Yantra symbol, which is oftentimes associated with Amma because it is an ideal symbol to represent her direct experience of the formless aspect of the Goddess.

It was during this period that Acchan resolved to join the thinking of his son Subhagan, that the Devi Bhavas should end once

Aum as it is written in Sanskrit

Sri Yantra: Symbol of the formless Goddess
The Sri Yantra's abstract symbol is a frozen wave pattern created by the mantric intonation of Aum. It is the most holy symbol of enlightenment in the Hindu Tantric tradition. It represents the formless Goddess—the feminine creative principle—"Aum."

and for all, and that family life be allowed to return to normal. After all, the family had suffered much as a result of his daughter's holy manifestations. The coming and going of devotees disrupted family life at the Idamannel compound. Competitive, business-minded priests from the various temples up and down the coast were complaining that Amma was causing them to lose money—since fewer people were attending their temples, and hence putting less money in their collection boxes. And his unmarried daughter continued the scandalous behavior of mixing freely with all kinds of people.

He beseeched Amma once more to give up her spiritual extremes.

"Let us be a normal family," he pleaded with her.

"We don't know who you are. Perhaps you are divine. But we are ordinary people. Let Divine Mother rest in heaven, and behave like a normal girl."

When this approach did not work, he decided to try another. One day, he entered the temple during a Devi Bhava and addressed the Divine Mother as she manifested herself in Amma.

"Go away!" he told her. "We don't want you to be here anymore. We want our daughter back, so that she may be married and lead a normal family life."

Divine Mother responded, "Is she your daughter?"

"Of course she is my daughter!" Acchan said angrily. "I want her back!"

"I will give you back your daughter," the Goddess conceded, "but if I do she will be but a corpse, and will soon be decomposing. You will not be able to give her away in marriage—you will have to bury her."

Not heeding her words, Acchan repeated, "Go away! And give my daughter back to me!"

The Goddess responded, "Here's your daughter, then! Take her!"

At that moment, Amma's body fell to the floor of the temple, where she lay motionless, with wide-open eyes. She did not appear to be breathing. Within minutes, her body began to stiffen, as if in rigor mortis.

A doctor who was in the temple checked for a heartbeat—there was none. Those present assumed her to be dead.

Acchan was overwhelmed at the sight of his dead daughter, and fell unconscious onto the temple floor. Devotees began to cry and sob. Others sat dumb with grief. It was unbelievable that Amma, who had just moments before been giving Devi Bhava, was now dead.

Hoping against hope, the devotees checked for signs of breathing or pulse, however faint. They found none. All hope of reviving Amma now gone, the devotees began a vigil, sitting near the body, which remained where it had fallen.

Acchan, coming back to consciousness some hours later and seeing the terrible scene of the vigil around his daughter's body, cried out, "O Divine Mother, I beg You to forgive me for the words I spoke out of ignorance! Please bring my daughter back to life! Forgive me!"

With these words, he fell down weeping. The floor of the temple became wet with his tears.

At first, the body remained still. But then, one devotee noticed a faint sign of movement. To the growing amazement of all those in the temple who witnessed it, Amma slowly came back to life.

When she was fully revived, she was in the mood of Krishna. She informed Acchan (who had been a follower of Krishna all his life), "Without Divine Mother, there can be no Krishna!"

Acchan never again tried to disrupt the Devi Bhavas.

Early in 1978, about a year after the death of his cousin, the bad-tempered Subhagan was not doing well physically. His legs had become afflicted by elephantiasis, a chronic and painful inflammation of the tissues. According to medical science, the disease is caused by the infestation of a certain type of worm in the lymph glands.

Although Subhagan went for medical treatment, his condition was not cured, and he became convinced that his elephantiasis was a terminal disease. He spoke of this belief to his friends and fell into a deep depression. Plagued by insomnia, he began to take sleeping pills. His dependence on these pills further exacerbated his depressed condition.

Subhagan continued his habit of treating Amma and her devotees with ill will. It was his practice to verbally abuse the devotees who came to the temple to see her, in an attempt to discourage their visits. One day, Subhagan teased and insulted a Muslim woman who had come to the temple for Amma's darshan. His words to her were so cruel and hurtful that the woman began to cry and bang her head against the threshold of the shrine room.

"Oh, Mother," she cried. "Is this what happens to the people who come to see you?"

Amma heard the Muslim woman weeping and came out to comfort her.

"Daughter, don't be upset. Daughter, forgive him."

Amma told the woman what she had told her parents a year before: that Subhagan was not long of this earth. "He has only days to live."

When word got back to Acchan of what Amma had said, he came to her in distress.

"Is it because of the way my son has treated you, that you are saying such a thing?" Acchan asked her.

"No," said Amma simply. "It is just his karma."

"Whatever he has done, please forgive him!" her father pleaded.

"I have not cursed him," Amma stated calmly. "I would never put a curse on anyone. Your son is destined to live only this long."

A week later on June 2, 1978, the body of Subhagan was found in his bedroom, where he had hanged himself. In suicide notes he left behind for his relatives and friends, he stated that he was unable to live with the pain and stress of his elephantiasis.

Damayanti and Acchan were devastated by his death, a grief that was intensified by their belief that Damayanti had contributed to his demise with her unsuccessful vow of silence. They also felt that Amma could have saved Subhagan if she had so chosen. Moreover, many villagers, as well as Acchan's relatives, blamed Acchan and his family for Subhagan's death.

Amma told her parents that Subhagan would be reincarnated in the family within the next three years.

"Don't be worried for Subhagan," Amma tried to console them. "He will be reborn into the family and become a good son."

In addition, she told Acchan that he would one day also get another son — not one related to him by birth, but a stranger who would come into his life, and whom he would come to love as much as he had loved Subhagan.

Reincarnation is accepted by Hindus as a fundamental part of how they view their place in life. It is understood that the deeds one commits (both good and bad) will bear fruit in the present or in some future lifetime. The soul, or what Hindus call the Self or Consciousness Principle, is enveloped by the causal, subtle, and gross bodies. The bliss sheath or the causal body, the subtlest layer, surrounds the soul. The causal body is then encased by the mental and intellectual sheaths, which together make up what is known as the subtle body. The causal and subtle bodies are then encased by the food and vital sheaths, which make up the gross atomic or physical body.

Reincarnation is a cross-cultural belief that was an accepted doctrine of the early Christian church until A.D. 533, when Emperor Justinian, for political reasons, had it declared a heresy by the Second Council of Constantinople. Basic to the doctrine is the belief that the soul, as spirit, never dies. At the time of "death," the soul vacates the gross atomic body, taking with it only the subtle and causal bodies in which are encoded the latent impressions of the person's good and bad actions. According to the Hindu scriptures, the soul reincarnates with its subtle and causal bodies into a new physical body.

Two years after Subhagan's death Acchan was anxious to marry off his daughters and arranged for Kasturi's marriage, which took place in September 1980. One day in early 1981, Kasturi was visiting Amma. Not knowing she was pregnant, Kasturi found it unusual that her sister held her hand on her stomach. While doing so, Amma repeated over and over the words, "Shivan, Shivan, Shivan." Kasturi took that as a sign she would soon give birth to a boy named Shivan. Amma informed Kasturi that the baby about to be born was in reality their brother Subhagan reincarnating.

On September 27, 1981, the same day as Amma's birthday, Kasturi gave birth to Shivan.

Acchan still tells the story of how he was playing in the sand with his one-and-a-half-year-old grandson Shivan, when the child suddenly told Acchan that he remembered hanging himself in a previous lifetime. Needless to say, Acchan was astonished.

Kasturi remembers that she and the villagers noticed that when Shivan was very young, he had many of the same physical and mental traits that Subhagan had. However, Kasturi said that these qualities only lasted until he was about six years old, at which time he seemed to take on a very different, and healthier, personality.

Shivan grew up under the watchful eye and compassionate love of Amma, who gave him much attention. From a very early age, she taught him to meditate and chant sacred songs. According to Kasturi, Shivan has turned out to be a very well-balanced and happy young man. The unusual circumstances surrounding her brother's suicide and reincarnation into her family only deepened Kasturi's respect for Amma. Kasturi said she no longer related to Amma as a sister but revered her instead as a great spiritual master and an incarnation of the Divine Mother.

Many people today can relate to Amma's family and the deep emotional pain they experienced caused by Subhagan's suicide. In the West, many disgruntled teenagers and those suffering from terminal illnesses feel hopeless and depressed and end up taking their own lives. In Amma's view, one cannot generalize about this subject.

She says, "People commit suicide for different reasons. Some do it because of family problems or failure in a love affair. In most cases, it is fear that makes one commit suicide: fear that their dignity or status in society will be lost, fear to confront a situation, fear that one might be killed by the enemy. And it is a weakness to commit suicide just because one is ill. Our life has not been created by us, but has been given to us by God. Past actions will definitely bear fruit," she believes.

"No matter how much pain you may suffer, try to think of it as a way to bring you closer to God, and try to cling tightly to God in such circumstances.

"The body has a sheath or an aura. Just as a tape recorder records everything we say, our aura records our every thought-vibration. And this recording remains even after we have died. When we commit suicide, we are causing the soul much pain.

"When the opening of a blown-up balloon is untied, the air in it is gradually released. But when we prick a balloon and it bursts, it explodes with a bang. So too when we forcefully end our own life, sudden pain-filled vibrations will be formed in our aura. This aura forms the basis for the next birth of the soul in a body. All that we are experiencing now is the result of our past actions. Understanding this, we should move forward in life, surrendering to God whatever we have to experience."

Chapter 6

THE TURNING POINT
HEALING OF A LEPER *(1979–1981)*

Neal Rosner was born in 1949 to Jewish parents in Chicago, Illinois. After high school, Neal spent a year traveling through Europe. On that trip he quickly became disillusioned with worldly pleasures, enjoyments, and everyday life in general. He came back to the United States feeling like a rudderless ship. At the invitation of his brother Earl, Neal went to Ann Arbor, Michigan.

When Neal saw his brother he was impressed by the positive changes that Earl had made in his life. Earl had become a vegetarian, and was now healthy and slim. Earl told Neal that he had been studying hatha yoga for the previous six months with a woman who had studied yoga in India under a master. She had also taught Earl about meditation.

Neal went to study with Earl's yoga teacher, and she gave him a copy of the Bhagavad Gita, a most revered Hindu scripture that contains the highest wisdom of the Vedic tradition. For the first time he learned that "the purpose in life was not to seek and enjoy sensual pleasures endlessly until death. Rather, it was to understand the mind clearly, purify it and go beyond it to experience reality where quiet bliss alone reigns supreme." Neal said, "For the first time since I was a little boy, I cried. Those tears were not born out of sorrow, but joy."

Earl gave him another book to read, on the life and teachings of the great sage of India, Sri Ramana Maharshi, who spontaneously became enlightened at age sixteen. Neal now realized that his purpose in life was to awaken to the same state of con-

Sri Ramana Maharshi
Before Neal Rosner met Amma he considered the great Indian saint Ramana Maharshi to be his guru. In the early days, Amma, along with her disciples and Neal, went on a pilgrimage to the Ramanashram.

sciousness that Ramana Maharshi had attained. At age nineteen, Neal traveled alone to Ramanashram in Tiruvannamalai, India, and took up the life of a monk. Although Ramana had left his body in 1950, Neal considered him to be his guru.

For twelve years, Neal studied with one of Ramana's great disciples, Ratnamji, who introduced him to other Indian saints. According to Neal, "A saint is someone in whom the Divine Light shines, who is experiencing the Presence of God. In Hinduism, there is no such organized way of proving someone's saintliness like in Catholicism. It is solely based on one's own intuitive feeling and experience of peace in such a person's presence. Miracles may or may not manifest."

During this time, Neal's health began to deteriorate. He went to all kinds of doctors—allopathic, homeopathic, ayurvedic—and tried all kinds of alternative treatments. Nothing helped. The doctors could find nothing wrong with him. One day, an astrologer told Neal that he might die some time in the next few years, or he would live and take care of his mother. He was quite depressed about this prediction, as he still had not attained the state of enlightenment that he had come to India searching for. A life back in America taking care of his mother was not what he had in mind.

By 1979, Neal could barely move from his bed, was unable to eat, and was close to death. During that time, a young Indian man approached Neal to find a place to meditate for forty days in silence. He told Neal that he had come from Amma's ashram and that Amma was a great saint and healer. Hearing this, Neal decided to go to Kerala to meet the saint, and ask for her healing.

Responding to Neal's request for healing, Amma said, "Son, everyone must suffer the effects of their past actions. It is due to bad actions in your previous birth that you are suffering now. But it is all ultimately for your good only.

"I do not think any doctor can find a cause for this sickness. It is coming from God to make you go higher in spiritual life. It would be a mistake for Amma to remove it. If you gladly bear the sickness as coming from God and cry to Him, fixing your mind on Him, then you need not take another birth.

"On the other hand, if Amma removes this trouble from you, you will certainly have to be born again and suffer even more than you are suffering now."

On the subject of how she knows when the suffering comes from God, and why she sometimes relieves suffering and gives healing, Neal (now Swami Paramatmananda) said, "Amma told me she gets an inner intuition that tells her whether or not to be the instrument of a person's healing. She can't go against that feeling, even if she wants to. In spite of all our efforts, if we still cannot alter our circumstances, we must take our condition to be the Lord's will for our own good. This is the attitude of the Indian sages."

Most of the time, Amma speaks in the third person—referring to herself as Amma or "Mother." Her use of "Mother" in the context of third person refers to the egoless or feminine creative aspect of God. A Westerner may find this way of speaking strange. But Amma does not identify with the body, or the "I" of the egoic personality. Amma once told her seekers that a saint's use of the word *I* is often misrepresented by followers of various religions.

She said, "No great soul will say, 'Only through me, you will be saved.' A real knower of the Self will not say that. After the founders of the various religions die, the followers interpret their teachings in different ways. Doctrines like, 'Have faith only in our religion' or 'Only through our path' are spread by followers who have no broad-mindedness.

"Do you know what the various mahatmas [saints] mean when

they say, 'Believe in me'? The 'I' they talk about is not the small 'I' which denotes the individual. It is that 'I' which is the Supreme Principle. 'In me' means 'in God.' When Sri Krishna told Arjuna, 'Have faith in Me,' he meant to have faith in that 'I' which is the Supreme Principle. But now, some Hindus say that you will gain liberation only if you believe in Lord Krishna; some others say that Shiva alone is the liberator. This is not correct. The Truth is that however we call on the Lord, whether it is Krishna or Christ, He will help us to attain the Supreme."

Amma had predicted to Acchan when his oldest son committed suicide that he would soon get another very loving son who would not be of his flesh. That other son turned out to be Neal Rosner, whom Acchan indeed ended up loving like his very own son. A monastic by nature, Neal was allowed by Acchan to stay on at the family compound to protect and serve Amma, which he did for many years. He was overjoyed to realize that Amma was the "mother" the astrologer had referred to.

At different times over the past twenty years, Amma has given Neal deep inner experiences of bliss. In 1990, he returned to the United States at Amma's request, to oversee her newly formed ashram in San Ramon, California. Four years later he took formal, monastic vows and was given the name Swami Paramatmananda.

During the earlier years, Neal got to witness and record for posterity one of Amma's more dramatic acts of compassion—the healing of Dattan the leper.

Leprosy, a disease that has afflicted humanity on every continent since time immemorial, has etched in human memory a terrifying image of mutilation, rejection, and exclusion from society. Leprosy is a highly contagious skin disease that flourishes mainly in the "poverty belt" of the globe. As of 1997, it was

Amma with Dattan the Leper

estimated that there were between one and two million people visibly and irreversibly disabled from leprosy.

Dattan was born and grew up in Perumpally near Kayamkulam in Kerala, some twenty kilometers from Amma's home village. When he was very young, he became a victim of leprosy. His own parents and relatives turned him out of the house. Finding no other way to earn a livelihood, he became a beggar. Begging for his food, he spent his days and nights in a temple compound.

As the disease advanced, his whole body was covered with

infected wounds, which oozed pus. Dattan said, "My eyesight was almost gone. In place of my eyes there were only two small slits. The hair on my head fell out. Nobody would give me any food. I was not allowed to travel on buses. I used to cover my body with a piece of cloth, but that would stick to my body and stink from the pus and blood oozing from the putrid-smelling wounds.

"Even fellow beggars wouldn't allow me to eat or sleep near them. Insects always flew around me, disturbing me. At the mere sight of me people held their noses and shrank away. I led a dreadfully miserable and despairing life.

"Then I heard about Amma. I went to see her one day, but no one would let me go into the temple. People told me to go away because I smelled so bad. But the Holy Mother, in the mood of Krishna Bhava, called me to come to her. She consoled me and treated me like her own child."

With somewhat reluctant permission from Amma, Neal used an 8mm camera to film Dattan's healing. At the time Neal filmed Dattan, the leper had been coming to Amma for quite some time, during which his body was gradually healed of open sores.

Neal said that at the end of the darshan, Amma would search Dattan's body for wounds. Finding them, she would press the wounds so the pus came out. Neal watched through the camera lens as Amma sucked up the pus and spit it out into a bowl—again and again and again. Finally, when it was all finished, she rinsed her mouth out and washed her hands—thus ending the darshan for the evening. Many devotees who witnessed this shocking sight vomited, and some fainted. It was an extreme act of compassion—both horrifying and deeply moving at the same time.

Sreekumar (now Swami Poornamritananda), a young Indian devotee, found the whole scene particularly disgusting. "To be

Swami Paramatmananda (Neal Rosner)

honest, I was horrified at the sight. I felt that it was too much—that this act of compassion had exceeded the allowable limit. As soon as the darshan ended, I made my feelings known. 'Amma, you are all-powerful,' I told her. 'You can cure any disease by your mere will. Why this gruesome display?' Smiling, Amma replied, 'Son, I don't know why, but when I see that son with leprosy, I simply feel like doing what I do. Perhaps you will be able to find out the reason from spiritual books.'

"Shortly afterward I read in a book that the saliva of a yogi or a Self-realized master has great healing powers, and can cure many diseases!"

Neal, on the other hand, felt he had learned a profound truth from witnessing Dattan's healing. He had heard a lot of people "discuss" the Vedantic truth that they were "not the body." But until Amma's demonstration, he had not witnessed anybody putting this truth into actual practice. He observed those around him being attached to their bodies, and therefore spiritually powerless to protect themselves from worldly dangers. But he saw that nothing fazed Amma, and he sensed her firm conviction that nothing would happen to her body.

Neal realized that Amma knew that her spiritual energy would not allow her to get leprosy from Dattan. He said, "That aspect of her fearlessness was another aspect of her compassion. She was quite beyond taking into consideration the superficialities of physical existence. Amma sees only the soul in a person—even a person who is just a lump of sores and pus."

After being with Amma, Dattan slept on a mat in one of the neighbor's huts for a few hours before going home. Amma warned Neal and the other devotees not to sleep on the same mat that Dattan was using, as there was a very real danger of contracting leprosy. She was deeply concerned that anyone looking at her touching him might think that there was no chance of contagion.

Today, Dattan still lives in South India. His eyes have opened and he can see clearly. Hair has grown back on his head. He can travel on a bus, and people are willing to talk to him and serve him food. Though the scars from this terrible disease still remain on Dattan's body, no more blood or pus oozes from them, nor does he smell. He is happy because Amma has given him a new life.

Acchan, like Neal, had witnessed many healings and the flow of grace from his daughter's darshan. But he had both fatherly and prejudicial concerns, because Amma attracted to their home so many different kinds of people, without considering their gender, caste, or creed.

Some of those who came were sincere seekers who wished to remain in the presence of Amma because they regarded her as an enlightened spiritual master. By the end of 1979, these seekers formed the nucleus of an informal ashram.

They were a small, well-educated group of young Indian men who grew up together in the town of Harippad: Balagopal (Swami Amritaswarupananda), his brother Venugopal (Swami Pranavamritananda), Ramesh Rao (Swami Amritatmananda), and Pai, plus Neal and Gayatri, an eighteen-year-old Australian woman who had come to stay with Amma.

Three times a week the young Indian men, all in their early twenties, would arrive by bus at the village of Vallickavu and then take a boat across the backwaters to Amma's home to receive her darshan. Recalling those intense early days, Swami Amritaswarupananda (Balagopal) said, "Every time we would go to visit Amma the villagers shouted all kinds of abusive words at us and even accused us of having an illicit affair with 'that fisher girl.' The villagers had no concept of pure, unadulterated love. Even the Ker-

Amma with early spiritual seekers, 1980
Standing left to right, Harshan (Amma's cousin), Gayatri (Swamini Amritaprana), Ammachi, visiting Westerner (behind her), Neal Rosner (Swami Paramatmananda), and Unnikrishnan (Swami Turiyamritananda). Sitting left to right, Ramesh Rao (Swami Amritatmananda), Satish (Amma's younger brother in front of him), Venugopal (Swami Pranavamritananda), Pai, and Balagopal (Swami Amritaswarupananda).

ala newspapers ran a series of articles falsely accusing us and Amma of all kinds of improprieties."

A number of other devotees and Balagopal were very resolved to put an end to these false accusations and so traveled three hours to the Trivandrum main newspaper office to meet with the managing director. It was their strong determination that finally stopped the fallacious editorials.

Balagopal came from a well-to-do and loving Indian family. However, his mother died when he was too young to remember much about her. His aunt, who raised him, and others from his village always told him how loving and kind she was. Growing up, he had an intense and painful longing to experience pure untainted love. "I continuously thought, 'Why did God take such a great mother away from me?' "

He had completed five years of college when he first heard about Amma. Although graduating with a B.A. degree in economics, his true interests were in singing and acting, two talents he excelled at during his college years. He was very involved with the college arts club and two of his great ambitions were to become a good singer or actor. Balagopal also belonged to the National Service Scheme, a student organization doing selfless service, and gave of his time to go to the slums and to help organize free medical camps. But Balagopal never once dreamed of becoming a monk.

At first he was skeptical about going to see Amma because the description devotees gave of her seemed so strange; they said she was possessed by Krishna and the Goddess twice a week. However, he was enticed to go when one devotee told him that they sing devotional music all night and that perhaps he would get to sing.

He thought that was a good idea because he had a desire to

Swami Amritaswarupananda (Balagopal)
*Swami, in addition to traveling with Amma on her world tours, has
authored a number of books called* Awaken Children, *which chronicle
some of the early years with Amma and her disciples.*

sing in front of people as a performer and it would be an opportunity for people to experience his singing talent.

But situations do not always work out the way one expects them to.

"The first day I met Mother," he said, "created a total transformation in my life. I found in her the pure love I had been searching for. Pure love that filled my heart and soul, the void and all the empty spaces. When I went back home I realized that my previous way of life was finished. My intentions and goals were now going to be different."

His grandmother used to give him three hundred rupees a month for his own spending, which was a lot of money (seven rupees to the dollar) in those days. But after seeing Amma, Balagopal gave up living at home and totally renounced worldly life. At the time Amma did not have an ashram, so he wandered from place to place like a monk and slept in various holy temples at night. This greatly incensed his family and all their love toward him dried up. His grandmother stopped giving him three hundred rupees a month and forbade him from seeing Amma. "My relatives even did special pujas [prayers] to bring me back home. It was a very difficult period. I even had to stand up to my father, whom I greatly respected."

The family became even more incensed when Balagopal's brother Venugopal (Swami Pranavamritananda) joined him a year later to be under Amma's spiritual guidance.

When Amma first heard Balagopal sing she told him his beautiful voice was for God. In the early days, while Amma gave darshan, he would sit all night long in the temple playing the harmonium and singing chants in the deeply resonant voice that is the passionate voice of a mystical lover of God.

At Amma's request, Balagopal later obtained a master's degree in philosophy as part of his spiritual training. In 1986, he became a brahmachari (celibate student of a master). Then in 1989, he was initiated as the first monk in Amma's ashram and given the name Swami Amritaswarupananda, which means the embodiment of immortal bliss.

Swami has been vice president of Amritapuri Mission and Charitable Trust in India since the ashram was founded. He says he has met many people with good spiritual qualities who have come to the ashram with the intention of renouncing worldly life. However, after living a number of years in the ashram not all have been able to keep up with such a rigorously disciplined lifestyle and so they depart. Although Swami has had the unique opportunity to travel all over the world with Amma since 1987 and has been privileged to witness her boundless love and compassion, he still finds her a completely incomprehensible mystery.

Acchan, like any good father who has been brought up with East Indian cultural conditionings, was opposed to having the young men, except for Neal, live on the compound near his three unmarried daughters. At his insistence, the Indian men were allowed to come only on the three darshan days.

By the spring of 1981, Acchan had married off the last of his two other daughters, thus opening the way for an ashram to be established. Because a foreigner cannot live in India more than six months unless he or she is attached to an institution for purposes of study or business, the ashram was officially registered with the government so that Neal and Gayatri could continue to stay there.

On May 6, 1981, the ashram was formally incorporated under the name of Mata Amritanandamayi (Mother of Immortal Bliss), the name given by Unnikrishnan (Swami Turiyamritananda), Amma's first disciple. From then on Mata Amritanandamayi became Amma's formal spiritual name as head of the ashram.

The original darshan temple and Amma's home, 1979
In May 1981, the temple and house officially became an ashram.

Acchan donated to the ashram a small plot of land near the family home. On it they built a tiny nine-by-eighteen-foot two-room hut so that Amma and Gayatri could live in one room, and Neal and Balagopal (Swami Amritaswarupananda) could live in the other.

An ashram is usually the home of a spiritual master who guides sincere seekers in leading a spiritual life by engaging them in spiritual practices and study of sacred scriptures. It is common practice for spiritual seekers living in an ashram to perform some kind of altruistic service while studying with a master.

Gayatri (Swamini Amritaprana) had a great desire to lead a spiritual life. When she first came to Amma in 1979 from the Ramanashram, she felt an instant heart connection and knew that Amma was the master she wanted to study with. For over twenty years she has selflessly served as Amma's closest personal attendant.

Gayatri spoke about the changes that occurred when the ashram became incorporated. "Although from the beginning, our days with Amma had been filled with spiritual practice, darshan, and selfless service, for the first few years there was no fixed routine. Everything happened more or less spontaneously, with each individual free to make his or her own schedule.

"However, Amma gradually began to stress spiritual discipline and regularity of practice, and we all noticed a formidable guru slowly rising within her divine personality. Yet none of us were prepared for Amma's announcement one morning, about eight months after the ashram's inauguration, that from that day forth the ashram would function on a strict timetable, which each and every ashramite would have to follow exactly. On days not following a Bhava darshan, we would have to rise by 4:30 A.M. to meditate for a set number of hours, and attend spiritual classes and *bhajans* (devotional singing), in addition to whatever other responsibilities we might have."

Having the nature of a monk, Neal found the changes very positive. "It was a great relief and even somewhat of a surprise to see Mother taking the reins into her hands. I started to feel more at home, and the atmosphere started to change from that of a big house to that of an ashram, full of spiritual aspirants engaged in an austere and dedicated life.

"While the life in the ashram was undergoing vast changes, circumstances outside the ashram were also changing. More and more people started to recognize Amma as a living saint or sage who had realized the Supreme Truth. Her unique universal love, patience, and concern for all became known. She was invited to all of the important temples of Kerala and received with honors."

Amma teaches her spiritual seekers to give up anger. She says, "Anger and hatred make humans blind, causing people to destroy each other. Everywhere in the world people are killing each other. But the real nature of man is consciousness. Man is God, but he has forgotten this. What a pity! What a downfall! What degeneration!"

Many people who meet Amma's monastics tend to project saintly qualities onto them. However, Swami Ramakrishnananda shared the following story of how Amma helped him to change his volatile, angry temper when he was a young man.

At the age of twenty, Ramakrishna, who was born into a high-caste Brahmin family, worked in banking. It was a number of years before Amma would let him resign his job and live at the ashram permanently. Swami said, "When I was working in the bank, a few renunciates who were staying at the ashram got more time to be with Amma and spend more time in meditation and do other spiritual practices. But for some reason, Amma asked me to continue the job in the bank. I was really upset and after some months I became very frustrated because among the renunciates I was the only one who was working.

"This frustration would come out in emotions like anger and impatience with the customers. I would get mad at them if they made a small mistake in filling out the forms to deposit the money. The union at the bank where I worked was very strong, and the management could not take disciplinary action on its employees unless they committed a serious crime.

"So people just put up with me somehow! But later at home after work I realized that what I was doing was not kind. Because I worked for a national bank my salary came from the public money. If they didn't deposit the money or do any business with the bank, how would the bank pay me? So then I realized that I should not get angry with the customers. I told Amma, 'When people make small mistakes, I get really angry with them. I know that this is wrong, but still I cannot control it.'

"Amma asked, 'If Amma sent somebody to you at the bank, how would you behave?' I said, 'I would behave lovingly, and do whatever is possible for them.' Hearing that, she said, 'So, from tomorrow onward, whoever comes to you, try to think that Amma is sending them to you. You will be able to do the work with more love and patience.'

"It took some time for me to really get that attitude. It would fade at times. But still, with Amma's grace, I was able to attain that feeling. Before long, I was able to get over the feelings of impatience and anger, and serve people with a peaceful mind and with more love. It made me think about Amma more, and enabled me to do my banking job with a more divine spiritual attitude."

In 1984, Amma allowed Ramakrishna to live full-time at the ashram. However, he found his old foe, anger, coming up once again. "Amma gave me the job of driving the van, and I used to go shopping for the ashram, along with doing my spiritual practices. Driving is really crazy here in India; many drivers don't follow the rules of the road at all! You are supposed to drive on the left side of the road, but a car coming toward you may suddenly cut over into your lane and come straight at you. One day a truck came onto my side, and I was actually pushed off the road. I got really angry, picked up a big stone, and smashed the side window of his truck.

"I was twenty-eight at the time, and when I got back I told Amma about the incident thinking she would appreciate my courage. But she did not. 'Oh my son, what if Amma had been in that vehicle? Many times we think only after we act. Think before your act,' she said, and I saw my mistake.

"I learned through association with Amma that we can all develop good qualities. Everybody has to go through this to reach maturity. Even though I became a monk, in the early years I had many feisty, unsaintly qualities. But over the years, I have slowly overcome many weaknesses through Amma's grace."

Chapter 7

THE HUGGING SAINT
THE POWER OF PURE LOVE

The warm night air was filled with the amplified sounds of Amma's ashramites chanting devotional songs. A huge twenty-by-twenty-foot video screen was broadcasting Amma live at a program site in Ahmedabad, India.

Ellen, an American on tour with Amma, stood watching Amma's bigger-than-life image hugging the throngs. An Indian man in his midthirties approached her, saying that he was a Christian and believed that only Jesus Christ was divine.

"He was angry," Ellen said, "because he had heard people at the program referring to Amma as a divine incarnation." Ellen, who had been raised Catholic, could understand why he held this particular point of view. She explained to him that many people experience Amma as a Christ, a Buddha, or an incarnation of the Divine Mother, depending on their devotion and particular religious affiliation, but that Amma herself makes no such claims.

Ellen further explained, "Amma says that her mission is to give unconditional love and compassion."

In response the man pointed to the large video screen and said, "But how can just a hug transmit unconditional love?"

By this time a group of Indian men had gathered around them to listen to the discussion.

"It is good to be a healthy skeptic," Ellen said, "but you can never know for certain how or if Amma transmits unconditional love if you only *think* about it.

"It's not a matter of blind faith. You must personally experience her hug to know the truth. Trying to discern the truth only from the mind or blind faith, would be like going into a restaurant and instead of ordering and eating the food, reading and eating the paper menu instead."

The men standing around listening to the discussion nodded their heads in agreement.

Four months later, Calliope Karvounis, a fashion photographer from New York City, experienced Amma's hug for the first time at the Universalist Church near Central Park. Gently wrapping Calliope in her arms, Amma pulled her head close and whispered in her ear, "My darling daughter," over and over again. It was obvious that Amma's hug made a deep impression on her because walking back from the darshan, Calliope had tears in her eyes.

"It was a very moving experience," she said, "because through Amma's embrace I got to realize the power of unconditional love in a physical way.

"Amma says that people are born to be loved, but that it is the one thing they never really receive." Even though people marry, they do not really understand each other's hearts; they are unable to give and receive that love, and are therefore not able to really love each other. There is always a lack of love. It has always been Amma's wish that her life should become love and compassion itself.

"If we give away some of our money, it decreases. Love, on the

Amma with children at San Ramon Ashram, California, 1996
Children everywhere are magnetically attracted to the Holy Mother.
Many times she can be found playing with them.

other hand, comes from God, and that love will not decrease, no matter how much of it we give away."

Amma says she is not here just for a certain group of people—she accepts everyone as her own child. When getting a hug, many of the local villagers near her ashram and other people from around the world ask her for help with health, jobs, family, and money problems.

In the early days, many of her monastic aspirants were critical of the villagers for coming to Amma with such trifling problems. Having left the world behind, the monks were mostly interested in the more spiritual concerns of awakening to their divinity.

Brahmachari Shubamrita, a young monk who acted as translator for interviews with Amma's parents and the local villagers, explained, "Sometimes we used to ask, 'Why is Mother giving so much time to the worldly problems of the local villagers?' Mother used to scold us, saying, 'Because some of you can understand what real spirituality is, you feel that all these problems are trivial. But if you see it from the villagers' standpoint, these problems are the most important ones. If Mother just gives them some higher advice, they will never accept it because they are not ready. So Mother has to really be concerned and try to find a solution to their worldly problems, and then slowly bring them to the deeper spiritual concerns. It is a very gradual process.' "

Numerous individuals have testified that even one hug from Amma creates positive change in their life. Swami Paramatmananda (Neal Rosner) relates one such story about an Indian army officer he met in 1998. "The officer told me he used to smoke three packs of cigarettes and drink a bottle of whiskey every day. He used to persecute everybody that was below him in his command, and he took great delight in making his wife and his kids miserable. The officer's wife, who was a devotee of Amma, kept asking him to see the Holy Mother. 'Why do I have to go and see her? I'm not even interested in spirituality,' the man said. But because she kept nagging him, he finally went.

"Amma just looked at him from a distance after which he felt drawn to go up to see her. She just gave him the blessing of her hug—and that was it! The man said he just started crying and crying and crying, and from the next day onward he stopped drinking, he stopped smoking, he became gentle and stopped persecuting people. He started getting up at four in the morning to chant the holy names of the Divine Mother. This all happened in one day!

"The officer asked me, 'What happened, Swami? What happened to me?' This man's whole personality was revamped in one night, and most people can't get rid of even one bad habit after forty years. And he hadn't even wanted it to happen!"

How is it possible that a simple hug can create such a dramatic change in a person? "Amma's hugs and kisses," the Holy Mother says, "should not be considered ordinary. When Amma embraces or kisses someone, it is a process of purification and inner healing. Amma is transmitting a part of her pure vital energy into her children. It also allows them to experience true, unconditional love. When Amma holds someone it can help to awaken the dormant spiritual energy within them, which will eventually take them to the ultimate goal of Self-realization."

Swami Paramatmananda says, "Mother is an extraordinary saint in the number of people she intentionally instills spirituality into—even to the extent of hugging every single person that comes to her. Basically, everyone is potentially what Mother is. Mother's presence is invoking that reality [of divinity] within that person."

The magnitude of Amma's healing embrace is truly enormous. Her devotees in India alone number well into the millions. In Calicut, in South India, during a five-day program, Amma hugs over twenty thousand people a day, and at the Amritapuri Ashram more than seven thousand people show up three times a week on the evenings of her Devi Bhava blessing.

On the occasion of Amma's birthday celebration in 1998, twenty-five thousand people attended. Meenakshi (Mary Van Nostrand), an American woman who is a devotee of Amma, was there at the time and witnessed the *miracle* of her giving twenty-five thousand hugs—nonstop—in one twenty-four-hour period. On her annual world tour to fifteen countries in Europe, the United States, Australia, Mauritius, Reunion, and the Asian countries Singapore and Japan, Amma hugs as many as two to four thousand people each day. In all, she embraces well over a million people each year. And if that weren't enough, the Holy Mother takes on some of their suffering too as illustrated by the following story.

When Swami Ramakrishnananda was twenty-four years old, and first living in the ashram, he got to witness firsthand Amma's physical suffering that resulted from taking on the illnesses of others. "Amma told us," Swami said, "that through her spiritual resolve, she takes into her body other people's bad karma and physical illness. Because of her spiritual power and strength, she said she undergoes only a fraction of what another person might have to suffer.

"In those early years, I saw Amma a few times after giving darshan, getting restless, coughing, and experiencing physical pain. One night all of us who lived at the ashram went with Amma to a devotee's house. Suddenly, Amma had a headache and her body became really hot with a high fever. I could see that she was suffering. That night I asked her if I could take some of the suffering from her. 'Amma, you are taking the karma of others and suffering so much. It really pains me to see you suffer like this. I would like to share some of it so you will be relieved of it.' Amma said, 'No, no, you cannot take it unless you have the spiritual power and spiritual strength.'

"But I was in no mood to yield and told her, 'I cannot bear to see you suffering like this. Whatever is possible for me, I would like to do—please give me some of your sickness, which I can also share. She refused—two times. But I kept on insisting and told her I would stop eating and go on fast. So finally she said okay.

"Ten minutes later I started having a headache and began to feel feverish, and experienced terrible body pain. Another five minutes passed and I was delirious, rolling on the ground and

Swami Ramakrishnananda assisting Amma during Darshan

shouting things that didn't make sense. The pain became really unbearable for me. One hour passed, two hours passed, and nothing changed in the intensity of the pain. By morning the pain was still intense and Mother said, 'Take him to the hospital.' I was in the hospital for a full day. Although the fever went down that day, I experienced great fatigue and was unable to work at the bank for two weeks. I learned from this how much suffering Amma undergoes taking on other people's illnesses."

Another time, Swami Ramakrishnananda was the recipient of Amma's spiritual power to spare him suffering. One day in 1984, while he was driving the ashram van to Madras where Amma was to give a program, he discovered eight or nine blisters on his arm. "That evening I went to Amma, and she looked at my arm and told me I had chicken pox. Amma said, 'In this condition it is not good for you to travel. Go back to the ashram, because even if you stay here there won't be anybody to take care of you because everybody will be with Amma's program.' So she sent another monastic to go back to the ashram with me. I was very sad because I didn't want to leave Mother.

"The next day I was supposed to leave and Amma said, 'Don't worry, you won't get more blisters. The sickness will go away soon.' Saying this she showed me her arm, and I saw a few chicken pox blisters on it. When I arrived back at the ashram I saw that five or six of the other monks had also gotten chicken pox. They had blisters all over their bodies and faces. But I had just ten or eleven blisters only on my whole body, and very small blisters—all because she took my chicken pox onto herself. And the few blisters on Amma's arm disappeared in a few days."

Besides taking on the illnesses and bad karma of others, Amma suffers many times from being handled roughly by her devotees. Swamini Krishnamritaprana, an Australian woman, has been up close to Amma for many years, handing her sweets to give to people during the darshans at the Amritapuri Ashram. She said, "I've seen Indians grab her because they love her so much. They are much more physical in their devotion than Westerners. When they are in her arms they just grab and squeeze her without thinking that she has a human body—they just see the Divine Mother.

"It has been hard for me to watch her being handled this way. I remember once I told Mother that I was feeling *so angry* at the devotees for the way they were grabbing her. Mother just looked at me and said, 'This is their devotion.' I left at that point because I just couldn't stand to see them physically hurting her so much. She puts up with it because that is her life, to put everyone else before herself."

When Amma finishes a long day of hugging, the right side of her face has a dark bruise. And her spotless white sari is soiled with tear stains, makeup smudges, and sweat. In the early years Amma would only give darshan three times a week because she was hardly known. As more people began to recognize her advanced spiritual state, Amma began to give daily darshans.

Swamini Amritaprana (Gayatri) said that as the crowds grow to enormous proportions Amma just keeps accommodating all the people and their demands. "Mother just wants to do the maximum that she can for the maximum number of people. The world tours are much more intense, because it is three months, nonstop, two darshans morning and evening of each day. It is *very* grueling! When we come back from the world tours, the rest of us spend three days in bed, but Amma is off the next morning, giving darshan again.

"We try to tell her she should put a day in between the cities. But she doesn't want to waste a minute. She has diabetes and now suffers from carpal tunnel syndrome from hugging so many people."

According to Dr. Ragavan, Amma's body defies medical understanding. Dr. Ragavan was born on Mauritius Island, a French province one thousand miles east of Africa. He studied medicine in India and England, then moved to France to specialize in spinal injury, and the allied fields of neurology and orthoprosthetics. A few years after first meeting Amma, Dr. Ragavan became a devotee and moved to the Amritapuri Ashram to do selfless service in her hospitals. In recent years, he has been one of a number of attendant physicians to Amma and has examined her for diabetes and carpal tunnel syndrome.

He said that Amma made it clear from the start that his service to her was *not* for his technical or professional medical expertise, but for his interior growth so that he could deepen his spiritual relationship with her.

Dr. Ragavan said, "She asked me to examine her and do whatever investigations and tests were needed, so I did them. But her physical ailments mystified me from a medical point of view. The closer I came to her, the more difficult it was for me to understand her.

"First, she doesn't have a normal relationship with her body. When I talk to other patients and examine them, there is a direct relationship between the person I speak to and their body. But Amma is different. I saw that many times during darshan, she was obviously in physical pain. I realized that she could, in one sudden flip of her eyes or by taking a deep breath, pull herself away from her body, and then for the rest of the darshan not appear to be in pain. She has the power of playing, of being or not being in her body, as she wants."

Amma has said many times to devotees that she is *not* her body, but the Self—pure Consciousness. For most of us our physical bodies define who we are. But the Vedantic teachings say that constant identification with our physical bodies keeps us ignorant of our true Self.

Dr. Ragavan asks, "How can Amma's body bear the stress and strain it does every day? For example, she is a diabetic. For a diabetic to be able to sit for hours without eating, drinking, and sleeping without adverse effects defies medical understanding. A diabetic has to be very careful about eating at very regular intervals, keeping track of the blood sugar levels, and passing urine quite often.

"A diabetic has to have a good amount of food intake, but I have seen her sit for fourteen hours without getting up at any time, and without eating. By going fourteen hours without food, it is not medically possible for a diabetic to maintain health."

In regard to her carpal tunnel syndrome the doctor said, "I made a few things for her neck, shoulder, and feet and told her to wear them. She listened and watched attentively while I explained how to use the braces and demonstrated how she should move her body and neck so as to lessen the pain. Then she told me, 'My son, in love there is no head or neck or shoulders or feet.' What could I say to that?

"What she does physically, a normal, healthy person could do for maybe one or two days, and then they would need a lot of rest," says Dr. Ragavan. "They could not repeat, every day, morning and evening, what she has done for the past twenty years.

"When I first examined her, she said, 'You won't find anything.' Her body seems to have adapted itself to her requirements. The problems that I would expect to find are just not there. Her body doesn't follow the normal physiological rules, that is sure."

Through numerous interviews it became apparent that Amma was healing people all over the world, on many levels: physically, mentally, and spiritually. However, she acknowledged that the Western world has particular needs.

"There is a need for both physical and mental healing in Western countries," she said. "But the more important of the two is mental healing. It is their minds that are causing people their greatest problems. Though there is greater freedom in the West, people also have twice the amount of a different type of suffering.

"For example, two people like each other and get married. Then, when one of them loses interest, that person has the freedom to abandon the other and walk out of the relationship. But if the person you leave still wants to live with you, isn't it true that he or she will be sad? A person goes in search of freedom by leaning heavily on his or her selfishness.

"Parents often live selfishly, caring only about themselves. And so, their children never get the love and reassurance they should be getting from their parents. Paradoxically, though Western people have more freedom, their hearts are becoming drier and drier. They go on burying their conflicts and frustration in their minds until it all finally threatens to explode.

"What people really need is love and mental healing. If we have the right mental attitude, our external circumstances will change for the better, then we'll have both a peaceful mind and a healthy body. Spirituality is the principle that teaches us to 'air-condition' our minds. Trying to correct our external circumstances is like trying to air-condition the whole world. It cannot be done.

"If we adopt the spiritual principles in our life, then no matter what situations we have to face, we will be able to deal with them in a positive way. We will develop the strength to overcome any ordeal."

Amma says, "Only a true Master can heal the mind. In the West, much money is being spent on therapy and drugs to help solve marriage problems, heal depression and other mental illnesses.

"People turn to experts to lessen their inner pain, but all the experts in the world—the doctors, scientists, and psychologists— are people who dwell in their own minds, within the small world created by their egos. As long as they themselves have not penetrated into their own minds, how can they penetrate into others'?

"As long as they themselves are in the grip of their mind and ego, how can they help others to get beyond the mind and ego? They too have deep wounds, just like you. Such experts cannot help you to heal your wounds and remove the pain."

Dr. I. C. Dave, retired research scientist from the Babha Atomic Research Centre in Bombay, had just finished giving a talk about Amma during one of her programs at her Mumbai (Bombay) ashram. Soon after, a medical doctor, named Vimal Kshetrapal, approached Dr. Dave to tell him how Amma had just cured him of depression.

Dr. Kshetrapal said he had been suffering a very acute depression for many months. He had been under the treatment of psychiatrists, but it was not helping.

He told Dr. Dave, "I just was in Amma's lap for two minutes, and my acute depression was totally cured! It disappeared permanently!"

Dr. Dave asked him, "Sir, without knowing what acute depression is, in clinical terms, how can you say that it has disappeared?"

"When I was in the lap of Amma," Dr. Kshetrapal said, "I was crying like a small child and Amma consoled me. At that moment I came out of the depression. I know it happened, because I myself am a psychiatrist. I worked as a psychiatrist in the United States for about fifteen years. Now I am back in India, and really very happy that I am cured."

Part 2

BY THEIR FRUITS YOU SHALL KNOW THEM

I have put all my hopes in women. I strongly feel that the ultimate victory of nonviolence depends wholly on women.

I believe the strength which women possess is given them by God. Hence they are bound to succeed in whatever they undertake.

MAHATMA GANDHI

Aerial view of Amritapuri Ashram, 1999

Chapter 8

A THOUSAND ARMS OF
COMPASSION
AMRITAPURI ASHRAM, INDIA, 1999

It is hard for a first-time visitor to Amritapuri to comprehend that the six-storied temple that is surrounded by numerous ashram residential buildings, some towering eleven or more stories high, was the original site of the tiny, two-room ashram. These new structures have been built on backwater "land"—"land" created by Amma and her renunciates by laboriously filling countless bags with sand and then dumping them into the surrounding swampland.

It is expected that whoever lives at Amma's ashram be celibate and perform some type of spiritual practice such as meditation and continuous chanting of one's mantra (the holy name of God). In addition, residents and visitors alike are encouraged to perform several hours a day of selfless service (karma yoga).

The pink- and pale-rust-colored temple looks like something out of an inspired vision. Twenty-four stone steps ascend from the sandy plaza floor to the entrance to the temple. There, two massive pillars reach upward three stories to support a platform where a life-size sculpture depicts Lord Krishna riding in a chariot while his disciple Arjuna reins in five white horses as they strain toward the heavens. Symbolically, the five horses represent our five physical senses, which must be controlled if we are to awaken to our true nature.

Inside the marble-floored meditation hall, and in front of pastel-flowered pillars that frame the center stage, is a statue of Mother Kali. Once, when Amma was in Calcutta, some devotees asked her to visit the beautiful Kali temple in Dakshineswar. After seeing the statue of Kali, the Holy Mother expressed a wish to have the same Kali statue in the Amritapuri Ashram. And so her devotees asked the family of the craftsmen who made the original sculpture in Dakshineswar to sculpt another.

Learning to penetrate deep within oneself in order to find the bliss-filled silence of the soul is a disciplined challenge at the Amritapuri Ashram. Every morning around four-thirty, thousands of black crows begin cawing maw, maw, maw. Shortly thereafter, as if on cue, all the different Hindu temples up and down the coastal waters begin blaring their various sacred chants through loudspeakers. Then, at 5:00 A.M., the Amritapuri Ashram residents go to the temple to meditate and chant the one thousand names of the Divine Mother. After meditation, a temple priest waves camphor lights and rings bells in front of the goddess Kali statue.

By the time the sun has fully risen, the world around Amritapuri is even a greater chaos of sounds. The hum-clicking of sewing machines in the tailor shop, the clacking of ashram printing presses, and the sounds of construction workers hammering and drilling metal, blend with the squeaking wheels of large hand-drawn carts. It is not uncommon to hear the ashram cows mooing, young children laughing, and the ashram residents and visitors speaking in Hindi, Malayalam, Dutch, French, German, Japanese, English, Spanish, and Italian. Every morning, a short distance away from the ashram, fishermen of the village can be heard chanting "Hey la, hey la, hey la, hey la" as they pull their huge nets in from the Arabian Sea. If you had any doubt that "in the beginning was the [creative] Word or Sound," you need only go to Amritapuri.

This place is definitely a spiritual training ground, where sincere seekers' minds are purified of their deeply rooted, negative tendencies and prejudices. Remya, the director of charities, said, "The world is pouring through the ashram gates every day. And that's part of our training. Even if a visitor walks into the office as a tourist, and knows nothing about spiritual life, and may be dressed all wrong for being in an ashram, we still have to show that person love and respect. Mother's arms are open for everyone, and she's training us to be inclusive and nonjudgmental."

Swamini Krishnamritaprana said the ashram is like a miniature of the whole world, but in a controlled atmosphere. "It's a place where you have to face and work through the problems that come up, because there's nowhere to run to. This fact is very beneficial, because people learn to work through their psychological problems more quickly.

"One of the greatest challenges for Westerners at the ashram is the lack of space and privacy. They have to share sleeping rooms with total strangers. Traditionally, Indians have never had the space or the money for separate bedrooms, so they are used to many people sleeping closely together on the floor."

Swamini said that the challenge for the Indians is accepting Westerners as their brothers and sisters, especially if the Westerners are not dressed exactly the way the Indians are. But she said a lot of wealthy Indians face the same challenges as the Westerners,

Amma and Swamini Krishnamritaprana,
United Nations Summit

Secretary General Kofi Annan invited Amma to give a speech during the August 2000 "Millennium World Peace Summit." It was the first time in history one thousand religious leaders of the world's diverse faith traditions came together with the goal to forge a partnership of peace with the United Nations.

Amma said, "Terrorism and violence against human beings in the name of any religion should be condemned at the international level and the appropriate strong action should be taken. Love is the only medicine that can heal the wounds of the world. Love is the very foundation, beauty, and fulfillment of life. Where love exists, there cannot be conflict of any kind; peace alone will reign.

because they are used to having their own rich food, and they are not used to sharing their rooms.

A definite requirement for the spiritual life is getting rid of desire for physical comfort. Swamini Krishnamritaprana said, "Mother is a good example. She is just as happy to lie down on a bare, cement floor as on a fancy bed — it's all the same to her. She has peace of mind in all situations. Someone once gave her a Mercedes-Benz to travel around in, but if she has to walk or catch a bus, that's just as good. Detachment is to use the things that God has provided, but if they are not there, or if they are taken away from you, you have to be able to surrender them easily."

It is not unusual to see Amma's father, Acchan, walking the ashram grounds and cheerfully speaking with various visitors or ashramites. So many changes have taken place on his original homestead since Amma was born, not the least of which is his own personal transformation. He and Damayanti said they learned much through all their difficulties.

"When I was a young man," Acchan said, "I had an angry disposition. I didn't have any compassion toward anyone. But now I feel that my inner being has been completely transformed and the old Acchan no longer exists." He said he feels blissful witnessing Amma's activities spreading all over the world, and her numerous charities, which selflessly serve humanity. He confirmed that everything his daughter predicted twenty years earlier has come to pass.

Damayanti said, "Amma's love has brought my family and all our relatives together. The relatives who once opposed us now are proud to be associated with our family." She said that Amma's brothers and sisters now help out with the different charitable works administered by the ashram.

Acchan and Damayanti no longer see Amma as just their

Amma with her parents, Amritapuri Ashram, 1998
*Top left to right, Amma's mother, her nephew, Amma, and her father.
Bottom left to right, Swami Ramakrishnananda, Amma's cousin, and
his wife-to-be getting Amma's blessing before their marriage.*

daughter. In the ancient Indian tradition of honoring a great saint
or mahatma, they now bow down to her. It is not unlike the
Catholic tradition of kneeling down and kissing the pope's ring.

Swami Amritaswarupananda, who has been with Amma since
1978, said, "This transformation in Amma's parents is perhaps
her greatest miracle. But it was a slow, evolutionary process that
took many years."

Many of the villagers who were once antagonistic have changed
too.

Forty-four-year-old Samban, his wife, Manorama, and their two
children live in a poor, two-room hut within one minute's walking
distance of the entrance of the ashram. The hut has no running
water or electricity, but it does have a small shrine, with a picture of

Amma, next to the doorway. For the past seven years, Samban has worked as a boatman for the Amritapuri Ashram. He ferries people, free of charge, across the backwaters to the little town of Vallickavu.

When he was twenty years old, he and his many uncles and cousins in the village had been members of the rationalist group opposed to Amma and her family. But now he is her devotee.

A number of years ago, Samban and fifteen other fishermen were in a boat far out in the Arabian Sea when suddenly a huge windstorm arose, and the sea became so rough that it overturned their boat.

He said, "We were all in danger of drowning. Even though we had been against Amma, at that moment we all started praying and calling out to her. Miraculously, the sea calmed down and we were able to reach the shore safely. But as soon as we were onshore, the storm came up again."

Ten years ago, Samban's wife, Manorama, became mentally ill. She went to many doctors and hospitals and took many medications seeking a cure, but to no avail. During one of Amma's darshans, Samban asked her for a cure for his wife. When Manorama went up to receive Amma's hug, Amma took her finger and placed sacred ash on her forehead. Manorama said, "After that I was completely cured."

Amritapuri Ashram is a center where Amma has a thousand arms of compassion stretching worldwide to help nurture human beings spiritually, mentally, and physically. To accomplish this, she set up the nonprofit Mata Amritanandamayi Mission Trust, which is run by her monastics and thousands of devotees from all over the world.

In a short period of time, the Mission Trust has established orphanages, founded numerous primary and secondary schools, and founded the Amrita Institute of Computer Technology and the Amrita Institutes of Engineering, Advanced Computing, and Management. The trust has also established over two hundred ashrams throughout the world, built the Amrita Institute of Medical Sciences, an eight-hundred-bed, state-of-the-art hospital in Cochin, and is in the process of building twenty-five thousand free homes for the poor in Kerala and other parts of India. The trust has established a monthly pension fund for fifty thousand destitute women.

Amma, who was denied every aspect of parental care and love when she was a child, feels deeply moved when she meets neglected or orphaned children. In 1989, her arm of compassion embraced an entire orphanage at Parippally, on the Kollam-Thiruvananthapuram district border. When Amma heard of the children's misery, she directed the ashram to take over the administration and financial responsibility of the orphanage.

At the time the trust took it over, there were about four hundred children in the orphanage. They lived in appalling conditions; the children were found walking in their own excrement. There was no sanitation, and no proper clothing or health care. The food given them was of the poorest quality—no better than what was given to prisoners.

In January 1999, when a group of devotees visited the orphanage, they found a miraculous transformation had taken place. The children were smiling and joyous, clean, healthy, and colorfully clothed. The monastics assigned to serve the orphans as part of their spiritual practice had lovingly built new buildings, landscaped the grounds, and helped to educate each and every child.

The orphans giggled and clustered around the visiting devotees, begging them insistently for pictures of Amma—for truly she is their only Mother. Later, someone from the group granted their wish by sending five hundred small pictures of Amma—one for each child. A few hours after the group had arrived, Amma came to the orphanage to cuddle and kiss the eagerly awaiting children.

According to Brahmachari Dayamrita, the money to run the orphanage comes from unsolicited donations given by various people from all over the world.

Amma teaches spiritual seekers to remember that by selflessly serving the poor, they are serving God, for God resides in everyone. Her all-inclusive vision is reminiscent of what Christ said: "Inasmuch as ye have done it unto one of the least of these my brethren, ye have done it unto me."

In February 1996, at a packed program in Mumbai (Bombay) Amma announced a plan to build twenty-five thousand homes for the poor, all over India. The first five thousand houses, she said, would be built mostly in Kerala. A quarter of a million people sent in applications for these homes.

In the autumn of that year, dozens of young men and women monastics left the Amritapuri Ashram to go into the villages throughout the state of Kerala. Their first assignment was to verify that the applicants qualified for the free housing. For many of the young monastics, this would be their first contact with the poor. They were deeply moved by the plight of the people they met, who had no food or medicines and who lived in pitiable conditions, sleeping under saris or in plastic tents. This inspired the monastics to go on serving the poor, even when they were exhausted.

It was a long procedure to qualify a person for a free home. Everyone in their neighborhood had to be interviewed. Preferences were given to people (from any religion) who had no source of income, and who were mostly homeless—such as destitute widows, women abandoned by their husbands, sick people unfit for work, handicapped persons, and penniless old people.

Once a family or single person qualified, the monastics build a basic, two-room house made of concrete blocks, which is then

Building a home for the homeless in Kerala, India
Brahmachari Shantamrita helping the Japanese devotees.

cemented over and painted. Amma insisted that these houses should provide only the bare necessities, so that they wouldn't attract people who were not destitute but who just wanted a better home. Therefore, no cooking or toilet facilities were provided.

Funds for building the homes come from devotees living in the United States, Great Britain, and other European countries. Along with the monastics, groups of Japanese devotees have come and donated their time and labor. It costs about 30,000 rupees, or approximately $700, to build such a home, and a bit more if land has to be purchased.

The project had its challenges. When the monastics first went to the sites to build the homes, they found the people for whom they were building the houses sitting idly by drinking, smoking, and playing cards. Most of the people did not appreciate what they were getting and even thought it was their right to receive a free home. One of the monastics explained that many in India expect the government to give handouts to the poor. The idea of unconditional service, he said, was still new to most of these people.

The greatest lesson the monastics learned from the project was that it was not just about building homes but also about learning to have patience, tolerance, and unconditional love for ignorant people. It is a supreme spiritual test to give love and selfless service without getting anything back—not even a thank-you.

However, since that time, Amma has stressed the importance of the recipients' participation in the construction, so that they can grow spiritually too. She said, "The recipients should be ready to give a helping hand, as far as possible. Even if they can't help financially, they should help physically. Only if they are involved in the construction work will they really find happiness, and feel that the home is theirs."

Brahmachari Tapasyamrita, one of the monastics who worked on the housing project, told a story about Chinamma, a poor, Christian Indian woman who lived in a very impoverished district that was accessible only by jeep or trekking. She suffered from several illnesses and had to spend all her money on medicine. She was so poor that she hardly had enough clothes. And to make matters worse, her abusive husband badly beat her and even tried to kill her by setting her on fire. She prayed to God to please send her someone who would love her.

She finally divorced her husband and married Narayankutti. They lived in a leaky thatched hut with Chinamma's son, who was sixteen. The boy never developed physically and couldn't walk. One day, he caught a fever and, because Chinamma lived in such a remote area, she and her new husband couldn't carry him to a hospital. He quickly deteriorated and died in her lap.

Onam, her new husband's friend, told them about Amma and gave them a photo of her. He told them they should pray to the Holy Mother for help. Together, they prayed ardently and, one day, out of the blue, Brahmachari Tapasyamrita, who was working in the area, appeared at their door. Seeing their plight, he told them that they could apply for a house. Narayankutti filled out an application, and the very next day bricks began to arrive.

Brahmachari Tapasyamrita said that Chinamma was profoundly grateful to Amma. Today her worldly circumstances have greatly improved. She is very happy with her new husband, her new house, and better health.

Although Amma only went as far as the fourth grade, she very much believes that everyone should have a good education, and she has built numerous primary and secondary schools throughout India that incorporate a well-rounded approach to education. Public education in Kerala is similar to that of the United States. It is primarily rational and materialistic—students study to get a job and earn a living.

Amma says, "The present system of public education inhibits creativity and places too much emphasis on materialistic gains. In modern education, traditional values, age-old wisdom, and advancement in material sciences is what is currently needed. Exposure to the insightful philosophy of India's ancient and vibrant culture, along with an awareness of each child's inner potential, will make children better equipped to boldly face the challenges of life."

At Amma's schools, meditation is taught to children at an early

Amma helping with construction work, Amritapuri Ashram
Amma teaches that a spiritual seeker needs to be humble and always selflessly serving others. As an example to her disciples, Amma participates fully in much of the labor that needs to be done. She has cleaned toilets, cooked and served meals, milked cows, and filled sandbags to create new land for the ashram.

age because meditation enhances memory, sharpens the intellect, and helps children become more focused on their goals in life. She says, "Meditation is a priceless gift handed down from India's sages. It opens up a person's creativity and joyfulness, so that life can become a celebration."

Amma's schools stress developing a child's creativity. She has established the Amrita Arts and Cultural Centers to provide training for students in various forms of Indian classical music and dance. For the first time, girls are also being taught Panchavadyam, the traditional temple music of Kerala. And at the Holy Mother's English Medium schools, there are cocurricular activities such as literary clubs, nature clubs, scouts, newsletters, chanting, arts and drama, computing, sports, and yoga—all of which develop the faculties and inborn talents of the children and provide a creative outlet for their energy.

Amma believes that most present-day technical education mechanizes people to the point where they lose their human side. To counteract this dehumanization, her trust has established the Amrita Institutes of Engineering, Advanced Computing, and Advanced Management, at Ettimadai, fifteen kilometers from Coimbatore.

A number of things make the Amrita Institutes unique. In addition to learning the most up-to-date technologies, the students are given information on yoga, meditation, and on Amma's teachings. As part of the curriculum, students take a course called "Self-Awareness and Personality Growth," taught by a yoga teacher. Students learn the life stories of the mahatmas, like Amma, J. Krishnamurti, Ramakrishna Paramahansa, Jesus Christ, and great people of the world like Abraham Lincoln. The course is to help the students understand themselves. They learn about human character and exactly what the mind is.

Brahmachari Abhayamrita, the director of the Institutes, says that everyone residing at Amrita is considered part of a loving "family." Unlike most schools, where the teacher teaches and then goes home, the faculty live on-site and are expected to be fully interactive with the students. In addition to teaching, the faculty are expected to pay attention to students' extracurricular activities, emotional needs, and even be involved with students' communications with their families. The concept of the institute is based on the ancient Vedic tradition of education. In ancient times, students lived with loving and wise spiritual teachers until they were prepared to go on to the next phase of their life of making a living and raising a family.

However, not all faculty are followers of Amma, and so to teach at the Amrita Institutes demands much more willingness to adapt to a lifestyle that is unfamiliar to most of them. In addition, the students and staff members take part in a service activity with the nearby villagers. There are programs for understanding and eradicating leprosy, tuberculosis, and AIDS. There is also a project of greening the lands, since the once thick forest has been deforested.

Most students who are not able to pay the tuition are easily able to get bank loans, which they pay back once they are employed. Those too poor to get a bank loan are provided a scholarship or are sponsored by those students who have left the institute and are making enough money to donate tuition. Through this sponsorship program, former students learn to be more altruistic and unselfish.

Brahmachari Abhayamrita is an educator, a problem solver, and an administrator to a school that has more than one thousand residential students from all over India. Inspired by Amma's educational philosophy, he has selflessly served to make the Amrita Institutes a reality.

The towering buildings of the Amrita Institutes are out in a wilderness far from any conveniences. Under Abhayamrita's supervision, the monastics and some paid laborers have so far erected over 350,000 square feet of building space, including both residential and educational buildings.

Abhayamrita said that when he first purchased the land in 1992, it had to be cleared.

"Since all the land was full of thorny bushes, it was a very tedious exercise that took one and a half months of hand labor. Every day we cut bushes, removed the roots, and burned everything. In those days, we didn't even have any sandals to wear, and with all the thorns, it was a real torture.

"We were the first people to inhabit this area. It was, in fact, forest reserve—protected land. So there were many wild animals: wild pigs, porcupines, foxes, and wild peacocks in very large numbers. In the mornings, we would hear the peacocks crying. And there were numerous deadly poisonous snakes—the cobra and Indian krait.

"Even now, there are wild animals here. Once in a while, an elephant comes out of the forest. The other side of the hills is actually the Silent Valley of Walawar Forest. It's part of Western Ghats [a long stretch of mountains], and runs from Bombay to Kerala. These forests are green and beautiful. Silent Valley is one of the most precious rain forests of India."

After the land was cleared, they had to wait two years before they were given permission by the Indian government to build the Institutes. During that time, Abhayamrita and a few others planted sixty acres of mango and coconut groves.

Once permission was secured in 1994, they began building the engineering college, and in 1996 the Amrita Institute of Advanced Computing. By 1999, the engineering college had expanded to include eight branches of engineering: mechanical, production, electrical and electronics, polymer, CAD/CAM, biomedical, communication, and computer science.

There are stories about great yogis and sages in the *Autobiography of a Yogi* that illustrated how they had highly developed creative powers. Most people in the West do not connect creativity and the use of creative powers with spiritual understanding and as part of spiritual growth. However Amma, who fosters creativity in others and who is highly creative herself, explains, "Because sages see the whole world as one, they develop the power to predict everything that is going to happen in the future, and thus use their creative powers to benefit the individual, society, and the whole universe. But creative experiments done by people who see themselves as separate from the rest of creation will lead to the impoverishment of nature, and eventually to their own destruction."

Deforestation of the rain forests, biological warfare, misuse of nuclear energy, and genetic alterations are but a few examples that illustrate Amma's point.

"In order to be truly creative," Amma says, "you must have the attitude of a beginner. To be a beginner means to maintain innocence and receptivity, for it is only in this way that we can truly and quickly develop our knowledge. But to be childlike or innocent doesn't mean to be a weakling—far from it. You have to be assertive and forceful if the situation so demands. Still, you should maintain the openness and receptivity of a child as much as possible.

"Our minds are not expansive. To make the mind expand and embrace the whole universe, we have to become like children. Our goal in doing new experiments and making new discoveries should be the understanding of dharma and spiritual principles.

"Our creative efforts should be based on love and compassion toward the whole world; only then will what we do really benefit the world."

Chapter 9

RELIGIOUS DHARMA
Reestablishing the Sacred and Moral Order

One of Amma's Brahmasthanam temples

"Your heart is the real temple. It is there you must install God. Love is the divine offering. Good actions are the worship. Good words are the hymns," Amma said.

Amma said that in ancient times there were no temples. The heart itself was a temple. But in India the idea of temple worship, she said, had degenerated into mere image worship.

The concept behind Amma's new temple is to teach people how to worship so that they will awaken to their divinity. The temple building and surrounding areas represent a person's physical and subtle bodies. And the temple deity represents the Divine Consciousness within the individual.

Amma's world mission is to awaken her children to their divinity by reestablishing true spirituality based on the legacy of India's great sages. Every human being, Amma says, has the capacity to become enlightened, no matter what religious tradition they come from. "There is a Krishna, Devi, Rama, Buddha, or Christ hidden within each one of you. The great masters are able to see that hidden Divine Light, which is waiting to break through the walls of the ego."

The great sages of India originate in the Vedic culture.

According to Vedic scholars and the most current archaeological findings, there existed in the land of India, around 7000 B.C., what has become known as the Vedic culture. It was ruled by enlightened sages and was a time of great spiritual advancement. The knowledge of God and the spiritual forces of Light, truth, and friendliness triumphed over the materialistic forces of darkness, falsehood, and ignorance.

The sages (rishis) were men and women who intuited and experienced great spiritual truths, which they recorded in Sanskrit verse as mantras (sacred sounds or "words" of revelation from God). These recorded revelations make up the sacred canons of Hinduism known as the Vedas and Upanishads. They are India's great spiritual contribution to the world.

The sages recorded in the Upanishads that the supreme purpose of human existence was to awaken to one's divinity. They taught people the spiritual science of how to turn within oneself to find the Truth—the Soul (Self). India developed as a holy land as a result of this profound spiritual understanding that was revealed by her sages.

During the Vedic period, people did not have to worry about struggling for physical necessities because the land was fertile and the climate temperate. This freed the people to turn their minds to understanding the great mysteries of life. Individuals learned to live selflessly and in spiritual harmony (dharma) with the cosmic laws of the universe because they understood that the supreme goal in life was God-realization.

In the West, the masculine aspect of God has been stressed. But the ancient sages understood that God also has a feminine aspect, which they call the Divine Mother—Shakti or the creative energy of the Universe. Hence, in the Vedic culture, women were held in great esteem and honored as a vital creative aspect of Divine Mother. They were acknowledged and treated as spiritual equals to men, and even took part in the priestly rituals. They understood that spiritual equality was based on the truth that the soul is the essence of who we really are—not the physical body that the soul inhabits to play a certain earthly role.

The sages made great discoveries in the fields of sound and consciousness, medicine, astrology, the physical sciences, and the sacred arts. The culture was so advanced that the ancient Vedas speak about three types of aircraft and how to make them. And the ancient Vaisesika treatises expounded on the relativity of time and space, and the atomic structure of matter—almost three thousand years before modern physicists rediscovered the atom and Einstein put forth his theory of relativity. However, today many of these ancient Sanskrit texts are indecipherable except to a few spiritually advanced individuals who are also very learned in this ancient language.

When most Westerners conjure up an image of a sage, they picture a very wise but old gray-haired man giving philosophical advice.

However, according to Swami Paramatmananda, being a sage has nothing to do with age or gender. A sage is more exalted than a philosopher given to rhetoric. A sage is even more exalted than a saint.

A sage, he said, is one who lives in a state of oneness and sees God in everyone and everything, as he believes Amma does. He said that Jesus Christ definitely lived in that universal vision of oneness, as did Ramakrishna Paramahansa, and Ramana Maharshi.

Saints, he said, are great souls who are still aspiring for that vision and who are very close to having it. Saints see God in some people, but not necessarily in everybody—and so do not have a feeling of equality toward everyone. He said that it is the degree of purity of their minds that accounts for the difference.

He said it's like a saint looking up at the sun. "Between the saint and the sun are some clouds. The clouds may be very thin and the saint can see the sun, but there are still clouds or just a thin mist. But as long as it's not completely clear between the saint and the sun, the saint can't see the sun as it is until there's absolutely no screen there. So purity of mind is like this."

In Vedic times, people were assigned four basic roles in society, depending on their temperament and on how they lived the dharma, in harmony with spiritual laws. The colors associated with these roles denoted the quality of a person's natural tendencies or spiritual energy.

The sages noted that people had the different spiritual energies for all four roles within them, but that one quality usually predominated. The roles were not based on privilege, but on duty. It was expected that a Brahmin would live a pure and austere life, whereas less was demanded from those fulfilling other roles.

Thus Brahmins (poets and priests), whose whole focus was on truth and living a spiritual life, had the predominate spiritual energy or quality of purity symbolized by the color white. The kshatriyas (warriors and royalty) had the predominate energy of will and action, symbolized by the color red. The vaishyas (merchants and landowners) had the predominate energy of trade, symbolized by the color yellow. One who was little interested in spiritual truth became a shudra (serf and laborer) and had mostly the energy of ignorance and servitude, symbolized by the color black.

The Hindu gods and goddesses were represented by exalted spiritual colors. Hindu sacred art depicts Lord Krishna, Lord Siva, Lord Vishnu, and the goddess Kali with beautiful dark blue or blue-black skin, symbolizing the energy of enlightenment. But the goddess Saraswati, who represents the spiritual quality and purity of learning, is symbolized by white, and the warrior goddess Durga, who represents the divine fiery energy that destroys ignorance, is symbolized by red.

In ancient times, the four colors (white, red, yellow, and blue-black) symbolizing the different energies of the One Absolute Consciousness were not related to one's skin color and given a negative racial connotation, such as has happened in the United States to African-Americans and Native Americans. Dr. David Frawley, respected Vedic scholar and director of the American Institute of Vedic Studies, said that when Christian missionaries came to India, they projected racist interpretations onto these four groups of people in order to win converts.

The caste system was not originally a part of Indian Vedic culture. Unfortunately, over thousands of years, this ideal of assigning duty according to temperament changed into the caste system, becoming a branding at birth that one could not escape. Children who were not gifted intellectually or spiritually became Brahmins simply because they were born to Brahmins; children with no aptitude for fighting became warriors, while children with intellect and aptitude were condemned to a life of menial labor simply because they were born into kshatriya and shudra families, respectively.

This would be like a Western family of medical doctors insisting that a child born into their family become a doctor, regardless of the child's temperament. The child would be forced to live, marry, and associate only within a community of other doctors.

According to Dr. Frawley, traditional Indian society did contain ways to advance in ranking. For instance when one became a swami or yogi, one had to give up caste altogether, but then the Brahmin was looked upon as *inferior* to the swami and yogi who had renounced the world. A Brahmin for the most part was as poor as a shudra, or laborer. The other castes aspired to be rich merchants or powerful kings.

As the Vedic knowledge was forgotten, foreign invaders ruled India. The foreigners, mainly interested in material gains and sensuous pleasure, began subjugating Indian women. The once fertile lands were ravaged and deforested, and interest in practicing spiritual truths declined. India's bright spiritual Light became eclipsed by poverty and the dark forces of spiritual ignorance and materialism.

According to the Hindu tradition, during different periods in history, when the forces of ignorance have become especially oppressive and eclipse the Truth, great sages and masters like Lord Buddha, Lord Krishna, and Jesus Christ have incarnated to reestablish the sacred, ethical, and moral order of their culture.

Over the last twenty years, many people in India have witnessed Amma building new temples and have recognized her monumental effort to reestablish the Vedic truths and moral order of the Indian culture. As a result, many Indians believe she is as great a spiritual master as Lord Krishna, Buddha, or Christ.

The following is an example of how she is reestablishing the sacred and moral order of her culture.

PALAKKAD, INDIA, JANUARY 19, 1999

Thousands of Indians gathered at the site of Amma's Palakkad ashram in southern India, where one of her unique Hindu temples was recently built. The atmosphere would be sanctified by a chanting of the thousand names of the Divine Mother, five times a day over four days, after which Amma would consecrate the temple.

The famous American mythologist Joseph Campbell wrote about one of India's ancient Hindu myths. He told how it was thought that great yogis received divine inspiration for creating Hindu temples through the practice of deep prayer and contemplation.

According to the ancient Vedic tradition, yogis meditating to receive divine inspiration is no "myth" but a spiritual truth, and it is being reenacted today in a contemporary manner by Amma.

One day in the 1980s she was riding in a boat on the Kerala backwaters with some of her close disciples. She shared with them a divine vision she had for building a new kind of Hindu temple that would help to reestablish true spirituality as a vital part of the Hindu culture. In April 1988, her vision became a reality when she consecrated the first Brahmasthanam temple in Kodungallur, in her home state of Kerala. Since that time, Amma has consecrated more than twelve new temples throughout India.

During the evenings that preceded the consecration of the new temple at Palakkad, Amma sang praises to God while sitting on a colorful stage under bright lights. Huge speakers filled the air with devotional music. A jostling crowd of about ten thousand people had to be controlled by the local police. A Westerner experiencing this for the first time, and not knowing anything about Amma, might think that she was some sort of East Indian "Madonna" rock star.

Many Westerners worship rock stars, sports heroes, millionaires, and movie stars, desiring their fame and fortune—hoping it will buy love, self-esteem, and freedom from suffering. But Easterners traditionally worship great spiritual masters.

Amma consecrating one of her temples

On the morning of Friday, January 22 the sun shone brightly as Amma stood on top of a special platform erected on the roof of the temple. Assisted by her monastics, she was about to begin consecrating the new temple. Ancient religious splendor was revived with the trumpet sounds of conch shells, pounding drums, and clanging symbols. An Indian man rode majestically into the temple area on an elephant ornately decorated in golden silks and colorful jewels. The elephant stood regally among the admiring crowds, and witnesses said that tears streamed down his face during the consecration.

Several hundred devotees were perched on the rooftop of the ashram building directly across from the temple and were able to watch Amma consecrate the top part of the temple.

Several of Amma's devotees stated that eagles always appear when she consecrates a new temple. Amma once said that eagles are devas (gods), and that their appearance at a temple consecration is an auspicious sign. The eagle is a cross-cultural symbol. In Native American tradition, the eagle is the highest symbol of spirituality. In the Hindu tradition, Lord Vishnu rides the eagle called the Garuda bird. It was an eagle who dropped a fish into Amma's lap when she was forced by her older brother to live outside.

At the precise moment when Amma finished the consecration rite by putting the third and last cone on the temple spire, hundreds of devotees perched on the ashram rooftop witnessed three eagles suddenly flying in a tight circle over the temple spire and Amma's head.

Next, Amma descended the platform so that she could consecrate the interior of the temple. Four of her strongest monastics, with great effort, brought a large, four-sided sacred stone weighing three hundred pounds into the interior of the temple and placed it on Amma's lap.

There are four sacred images on the stone, which represent unity in diversity. This temple stone has no precedent in India's religious art, or in the known religious art of the world. It is unique to Amma's vision. Each symbol is meant to teach us to see the one God in all forms, especially in ourselves.

One side has the image of the Goddess (the feminine aspect), which represents the supreme power of God, by whose grace we are brought to the spiritual path. Opposite it is the image of Lord Shiva (the masculine aspect), which represents nondual Supreme Consciousness, which purifies spiritual seekers of their bad karma and bestows on them the ability to distinguish between good and evil. The elephant god Ganesh, on the third side, represents that aspect of God that removes the obstacles from the seeker's spiritual path. On the fourth side is an image of a serpent that represents Kundalini Shakti, the serpent power lying dormant in the seeker's first chakra, which when awakened by one's spiritual practices results in awakening to one's divinity.

Inside the temple, before the stone was installed, Amma had consecrated nine gems representing the nine planets and the sun—a ruby, pearl, coral, emerald, yellow sapphire, diamond, blue sapphire, cat's eye, and garnet. These she had placed in a precise astrological configuration in the base of the foundation where the stone was to be installed. After that a specially consecrated Sri Yantra symbol made out of metal was placed on top of the jewels.

Amma then performed ancient tantric rites, similar to Tibetan Buddhist rituals. She purified the stone by imbuing it with *pranic* (life force of Shakti) energy. At that moment, the Palakkad temple became a sacred place that emanated a beneficial spiritual power.

Brahmachari Dayamrita has helped carry sacred stones into various new temples for installation. He said that although it takes four men to carry it, Amma, at a certain point in the ritual, takes the stone, which they have placed on her lap, and using only her hands, she easily lifts it into place as if it weighs nothing. This of course continues to amaze him and the other swamis. However, it is known in India that great yogis or sages can have spiritual powers to make even heavy objects weightless.

The great saint Sri Ramakrishna Paramahansa once said that when a mahatma or great soul comes to earth, many sciences such as pujas and Vedic astrology are revived. Amma is revitalizing these sciences within her ashrams. That evening, seven thousand people took part in what is known as a Saturn puja, led by the Holy Mother. Pujas are special spiritual practices to alleviate human suffering.

They consist of rituals and sacred mantras that can help alleviate some of the negative effects that a person is due to suffer because of his or her past misdeeds. It is similar to having a special series of Catholic masses or a rosary novena said to help a person who is going through a hard time.

Pujas are based on Vedic astrology, which is considered an intuitive spiritual science in India. By having one's Vedic astrology chart done by a competent astrologer, a person can know what bad influences are occurring as a result of past karmic transgressions. The astrologer then can recommend the performance of specific pujas to lessen these negative influences.

Normally, only male Hindu priests have done pujas. But Amma is teaching all people to take an active part in doing group pujas. She says much more grace is generated when people pray and do the ritual together.

That evening, after the temple consecration, the seven thousand people gathered for the Saturn puja sat one person across from another, in rows so tight that no one could move.

In front of each person was an incense stick, a small clay pot filled with water and wrapped in palm leaves, a betel leaf, a betel nut, and a tiny camphor lamp. As the puja progressed, the warm night air was permeated with the odor of incense and the flickering light from seven thousand tiny camphor lamps.

As part of the ritual, the people symbolically placed all their bad karma in the water pot. Then they circled the camphor lamp three times above their heads while chanting Om (Aum) and other mantras. At the end, they all held the water pot over their heads and went to the new temple. There, puja priests would take their "karma-infested" water and pour it over the newly consecrated temple stone, thus neutralizing the harmful and negative effects in their lives.

At that moment, two Americans who attended the puja experienced a new level of understanding of unity in diversity. Linda and Bob Knickerbocker got caught up in the swarm of seven thousand people moving toward the tiny temple. They were jammed so tightly against other people that they could hardly breathe. They went to a safe spot inside the temple gate where they stood looking out at the sea of faces holding water pots over their heads. Linda said, "It looked like one coherent body, composed of thousands of heads and thousands of intense eyes, moving as one gigantic wave of primal energy."

In November 1997, the following headlines in Kerala's newspapers caught the attention of the people: KERALA WOMEN PRIESTS PRACTICE SPIRITUAL EQUALITY AND WOMEN PRIESTS IN KERALA END MALE MONOPOLY. Amma had challenged traditional Hinduism by allowing priestesses to take charge of two of her temples, in Kaimanam and Kodungalloor.

Although a number of Hindu priests and scholarly pundits voiced opposition, Amma boldly did what no other enlightened female Hindu had ever done. She consecrated a number of new temples and empowered her women renunciates to study and become pujarinis, or priestesses. In her effort to reestablish the pure Vedic tradition, she told her disciples that it is not enough to just preach liberty for women. It has to be practiced and demonstrated.

Authorities had expected trouble and public protests, but instead more people came to her temples than ever before.

One Vedic scholar and priest, Mr. Vishnu Narayanan Namboodiri, supported Amma by saying that women priestesses were just as competent as men. He said there was no Vedic sanction for male domination and the subjugation of women, and cited instances in epics and ancient literature that showed women as equals to men. He said that Amma was rectifying the bad aspects of history, tradition, and superstition that have kept women down.

It all started one day when Amma asked her male disciples who were Hindu scripture scholars to find out if it was written anywhere in the scriptures that women could not be priests. They searched

Bramacharinis learning to be pujarini priestesses

and searched and reported back to her what they had found. She told them that certain scriptural words they pointed out were mis-interpreted so as to suggest that only men could be priests, and that therefore there was nothing in the scriptures saying that women shouldn't be priests.

At that moment, Amma asked her female disciples how many would like to study to become priests. A number of them raised their hands. Much to the initial distress of her male disciples, Amma directed the women to study the rituals and scriptures for three years, in preparation to serve as priests in her new temples.

Asked her opinion on the current controversy in the West about Christian women becoming priests, Amma said, "I will never speak ill of the rules of any religion. But I do not believe that Christ actually said that only men should become priests. God sees everything as One. How can we call someone 'God' who looks upon men and women as unequal, and who doesn't see the same Divine Principle in everyone?

"So it isn't likely that Christ would have said such a thing. Tra-ditionally, only men used to go out to work. Women used to stay at home, take care of the children, and look after the household. That may be how this practice of only men being priests came into being.

"In the eyes of God, men and women are equal. How can one possibly justify saying that a women, who is the creator of man, is inferior to man?"

Buddhist monks, Catholic priests and nuns, Muslims, Jews, and people from numerous other religious traditions have gone to the Holy Mother to receive her blessing of unconditional love. Although she is reestablishing the Vedic tradition in India, she is not trying to make converts out of those who come to her. She honors and blesses all traditions. In fact, many who come to her in the West are Christians and Jews who have asked her to initiate them into a sacred mantra. She will give them a mantra according to their own religious tradition, such as a mantra for Christ or the Virgin Mary. Muslims may ask her for a mantra honoring Allah. She cares only that individuals grow in the love of God, and see God in everyone.

Many wars have been fought over religion, and untold suffering has resulted. In answer to the question of what can be done to help people understand the unity underlying all religions, Amma said, "In today's world, religion has become merely ritualistic, and the fundamental principles behind religion have been forgotten. The basic, underlying principle of all religions is one and the same Truth. Different religions are suited to different people for their spiritual development, and therefore no one religion is superior to any other.

"A manager once appointed four people to plant a tree. One was to dig a hole in the ground, one to plant seeds in the hole, one to water the seeds, and the fourth to fill the hole with soil. But the person who was supposed to plant the seeds never turned up. Still, the three others did what they had been told to do. A fence was then built around the area. But of course no tree ever grew out of the patch of soil.

"Most of the preachers of the different religions are like the men in the story. They are ignorant of the underlying principles and purpose of religion. They focus only on the superficial aspects of their religion; they do not even bother to practice the teachings of their faith."

Different religions, she said, have become like business companies trying to increase their sales by competing with one another, because they view all other religions as their enemies.

She said, "We are like chocolates wrapped in different col-

**Abbot Lobsang Dorje Rimpoche, Amma, and Monsignor Vigile,
bishop of the French Orthodox Church, France, 1998**
(Courtesy of Father Basile.)

During Amma's European tour, Bishop Vigile and Tibetan monk Lobsang Dorje shared an hour of communion with her. Monsignor Vigile said, "The French Orthodox Church favors more and more these simple meetings and exchanges between the great (spiritual) traditions. With Amma, it was more than that, it was a meeting of the hearts."

Lobsang Dorje honored Amma by singing to her the Buddhist chant "Praise to Tara." Tara is the main feminine divinity in the Buddhist tradition.

Amma, well respected in religious circles, was named one of three presidents of Hinduism by the 1993 Parliament of the World's Religions in Chicago, Illinois. In 1995, she was a keynote speaker for the United Nations' Interfaith Council in celebration of its fiftieth anniversary.

ored wrappers. When the wrappers are removed, all the chocolate is the same. If we light a green and a blue candle, the flames
will be the same color. The nectar of different flowers is all the
same to the honeybee. And though the shapes of ice may differ,
it is all just water. So too everyone in this world is the one Atman
[Soul]. We are all are God's children."

Chapter 10

SAINTS, SAGES, AND SCIENTISTS

Mumbai (Bombay) Scientists Study Amma

In the beginning of the twentieth century, physicists uncovered the secret of how to release the energy of the atom. Since that moment, our world has not been the same. Applied physics research has produced amazing scientific technologies that can be used to either advance or destroy civilization and all life on earth.

Most Western scientists believe that a logical and rational approach to research is the only way to learn the truth about ourselves and the Universe.

The science of physics, for example, depends on mathematical theory and objective analytical experimentation. The "truth" about the nature of the Universe is gained primarily by a scientist coming to an intellectual conclusion based on mathematics and the data produced from experiments using scientific equipment, such as a cyclotron. This data is then transferred to the mind of the scientist through his or her physical eyes, and depending on the experiment, through other physical senses as well (hearing, taste, touch, and smell). However, when great scientific discoveries are made, the solution or insight to the problem usually comes first as an intuitive flash—like Einstein's theory of relativity.

(*Courtesy of European Southern Observatory.*)
Amma told her young disciples that the "real scientist" is the sage who experiments in the inner laboratory of the soul and experiences life and love everywhere—even in hell, even in the nether world.

"While the scientist burdens himself with facts and figures, the Sage becomes empty so that all knowledge can pass through him without it affecting his experience of Oneness.

While the scientist limits and narrows his vision, the Sage expands and embraces the entire universe.

The scientist sees many—the Sage sees One.

The scientist is only a part of existence, while the Sage is the whole of existence."

—Amma

In 1984, during the early days of the ashram, a number of young Indian men who had a deep interest in science and who were also spiritual seekers, approached Amma with questions regarding its importance. She told them, "Science is growing, but the human heart is shrinking. Too much intellectualizing and reasoning has killed the beauty and charm of life. Human beings have lost faith in their own soul. They do not know who they really are. Our overindulgent and intellectual approach to life is soon going to pave the path for our destruction.

"What we really need is a discriminating intellect—to discriminate between good and bad, and a compassionate heart, in order to feel and express love.

"A scientist may claim he is trying to find the truth of the empirical world through an analytic approach. He dissects things to analyze how they function. If he is given an animal, he is more interested in using it for research than in loving it as a pet. He will measure its rate of breathing, its pulse and blood pressure. In the name of science and the search for truth, he will dissect the animal and examine its organs.

"Once it has been cut open, it is dead.

"In his search for the truth of life, the scientist unwittingly destroys life itself! Life is love—a real scientist should love mankind and all of creation."

Albert Einstein, Time magazine's choice for man of the twentieth century, in essence felt the same concerns as the Holy Mother when he said, "We shall require a substantially new manner of thinking if mankind is to survive."

By 1986, Amma was making plans to go on her first world tour. In preparation for the first segment of the tour, monastics made arrangements to host her in various cities in North India.

Scientists of the Bhabha Atomic Research Centre in Mumbai (Bombay) agreed to host Amma's program at the research center's residential complex. Six months prior to her first visit, the monastics sent a video of the Holy Mother to the Research Centre.

Dr. I. C. Dave, a well-respected, retired, senior scientist in radiation biology, recalls that he and sixteen other scientists and engineers became intensely absorbed in the video. There was something highly unusual about it.

The scientists sat for a few moments in thoughtful silence after the video was over. Breaking the silence, one of them asked, "Did any of you observe the way the image of Amma seemed to be projected as a three-dimensional figure right into this room?" All the other scientists agreed that they had seen the same thing. Each had been silently thinking that they were experiencing an illusion.

After some discussion their trained inquisitive minds went from observation to analysis. What was the scientific principle behind what they had experienced? When they were not able to immediately determine this, they decided that Amma was a person who could possibly teach them something in the field of science.

Others have experienced a similar phenomenon. When Amma is not physically present at the San Ramon Ashram in the United States, devotees place a framed photograph of her in the chair she normally sits in. One day in October 1998, Stella Petrakis, from San Francisco, California, using ordinary film and a disposable camera, photographed Amma's framed picture in the chair. In this photograph, Amma's head appeared to be projecting three dimensionally outside the framed photograph (see the illustration on the next page).

Amma's photograph in her chair
(Courtesy of Stella Petrakis, 1998.)

Dr. Dave, a deeply spiritual man, had practiced transcendental meditation for many years before his first meeting with Amma.

Six months after seeing her video, he met Amma for the first time. With a beautiful smile she greeted Dr. Dave in a most familial way, saying, "I am your mother. We have been together in many lifetimes. You don't remember anything; I remember everything." Dr. Dave said, "I was stunned because what she said to me reminded me of what Lord Krishna had told Arjuna in the Bhagavad Gita."

Dr. Dave further said, "And then she started giving experiences after experiences to each one of us, in such a wonderful way, that our faith in Amma strengthened, and our interest as scientists started growing."

Because of the Mumbai scientists' increasing interest in Amma, a special retreat was arranged for November 28, 1987, at Lonavla, a small hillside town between Bombay and Pune. This exclusive get-together included thirty scientists from the Bhabha Atomic Research Centre, Amma, and a few of her monastics.

Dr. Dave said that a discussion in relation to time and space was initiated by Dr. D. N. Srivastava, a physicist and research officer. Dr. Srivastava received his degrees in medical science and physics from the University of Gorakhpur, and a Ph.D. in physics from the University of Bombay.

Amma told Dr. Srivastava, "Basically, time is not linear. Space is not linear. It is circular."

"At that time, we scientists could not follow what Amma was trying to tell us," Dr. Dave said. "But later on we came to understand what she was referring to. According to our understanding of Amma, she was referring to time not in terms of minutes, months, or seasons. She was saying that time has to be understood in terms of the circle of life and death. It's a circle, or a cycle."

Dr. Srivastava's interest was in developing a theory of physics

Dr. I. C. Dave

Dr. Dave has degrees in chemistry, botany, and plant physiology and joined the Bhabha Atomic Research Centre in 1967. Since retiring from the Research Centre in 1995 he has been giving lectures on the synthesis of science and religion and conducting programs on meditation and yoga.

and mathematics based on the Hindu spiritual science of Vedanta, which asserts that there is only one Creator (monotheism) from which everything else ensued.

Dr. Srivastava began by asking Amma a very simple question: "Amma, according to modern physics, fundamental particles are the basic constituents of the entire universe. We understand the nature of fundamental particles with the help of different systems. We can study them theoretically, and then make predictions about the behavior of these particles, which can then be verified through experiments done in machines like cyclotrons and particle accelerators."

When Dr. Srivastava was about to elaborate, Amma interrupted him, saying, "Your machines, which help you study the fundamental particles—they themselves have limitations. How can a thing that has limitations give you the full understanding?"

How can a machine that has limitations give you the ultimate truth? The scientists were taken aback.

Amma then stated, "You scientists are wasting your time and money!"

Dr. Dave said the scientists sat silent and stunned because they knew she was right! None of them had thought that a simple thirty-four-year-old saint from a poor remote fishing village in Kerala would know anything about science—but they were in for more surprises.

Because of his interests in biology, Dr. Dave asked the Holy Mother to clarify some issues concerning evolution.

"Amma," he said, "physics is concerned with the properties of matter, but biology is a science of a living system. As far as a biologist is concerned, the basic unit for manifestation of life is identified in terms of a chemical, called DNA, which is supposed to contain all the information about the growth and physiology of the body.

"We can have a lot of DNA in a test tube, but we cannot create life out of it. We still need to use chemicals derived from living systems.

"How can we bring life into a DNA molecule? Can we do it or not? What is that particular element of life that is different from matter?

"I was stunned when she said, with a lovely smile, 'My dear son, you scientists have a lot of drawbacks. One of these drawbacks is that your knowledge is confined to the realm of only three dimensions.' "

Dr. Dave was particularly excited to hear Amma use the word *dimensions*. When scientists think of dimensions, in regard to the physical world, it is in terms of the three dimensions of space (length, breadth, and height) and time, which is often referred to as a fourth dimension (space/time).

Needing clarification he asked, "Amma, if you say that our knowledge is confined to only three dimensions, there must be others. What are they?"

She explained that the "three dimensions" she was referring to were those of the sleeping, waking, and dream states—not those of space or time.

Amma said, "In the sleep and dream state you don't know anything. When you are awake, your knowledge is confined to a very limited understanding of nature.

"Physics is only part of nature, not the whole. So whatever you understand with the help of physics is very limited."

Dr. Dave asked Amma to tell him how many "dimensions" she knew there were. She said, "There are nine dimensions." Dr. Dave then asked her to name them.

Amma said, "The 'fourth dimension' is known to everybody as the state of samadhi [uniting one's soul in deep meditation with the Supreme Consciousness called God, or Brahman]."

Amma then became very serious. "Even if I reveal the smallest fraction of my fourth dimension, you won't be able to face me at all," she told him.

Dr. Dave said he became a bit frightened. He later said, "I think what Amma was trying to say is that her 'fourth dimension' would be glowing with immense energy. Her statement very clearly showed me that Amma is not just what we see, and I learned from her that it is important for one to have knowledge of the 'fourth dimension' through the profound subjective experience of samadhi."

Not unlike Amma, Saint Hildegard of Bingen and Saint Thomas Aquinas, two great saints from the West, also affirmed that more inclusive knowledge of the whole universe is already within us, but is only revealed through deep inner meditative experiences.

Saint Hildegard was a twelfth-century Benedictine abbess and spiritual genius from Germany who testified that all her extensive knowledge of science, music, medicine, and herbology came through revelations from God during her profound inner states of contemplation. Saint Thomas Aquinas, considered a great intellect of the Catholic Church, one day while writing on doctrine had a deep mystical experience. This inner revelation so transformed his mind that he made a declaration before he died that everything he had written so far was like so much straw — worthless.

Dr. Dave arranged for this author to interview his friends Dr. I. V. V. Raghavacharyulu, a retired senior research physicist, and Dr. Srivastava. We met at Dr. Srivastava's apartment at the Research Centre.

They enthusiastically responded to the first topic of discussion — the Sri Yantra symbol — signifying the merging of the

Detail of the metal Sri Yantra symbol
The inscriptions on the metal Sri Yantra are mantras or sacred sounds written in Sanskrit. Such sounds were originally revealed by the great sages of India.

Hindu sacred art and science of sound and consciousness. Symbolizing the primal sound of Aum or creative principle of the universe, the Sri Yantra is composed of nine overlapping triangles of various sizes. These triangles are then surrounded by a circle of eight petals, a circle of sixteen petals, and three other concentric circles contained in what looks like a cross.

The Sri Yantra symbol is usually made of either copper, silver, or gold and has Sanskrit mantras written on the lines and petals of the design (see page 67). According to the Hindu Tantric tradition, the sound of a mantra corresponds to a specific vibrational pattern called a yantra. Thus, the Sri Yantra is the vibrational pattern created from the mantric sound of Aum.

Based on the 1970s pioneering sonic research by Swiss scientist Hans Jenny, Deepak Chopra, M.D., in a video titled *Of Sound Mind and Body*, illustrated how when one intones the mantra Aum, on a flowable fluid such as oil or water, an oscillating Sri Yantra wave pattern is created. A simple experiment will suffice to help you visually understand this concept. Take a small bowl of water and let it rest until the water is calm as glass. Then, without touching the bowl, blow on the water.

Hans Jenny echoed the teachings of the ancient sages when he said, "The more one studies these things, the more one realizes that sound is the creative principle. It must be regarded as primordial."

Each of the three scientists felt the Sri Yantra symbol held great significance for science. Dr. Raghavacharyulu felt that it contained "a fantastically important mathematical theorem." He said the sages were the first people who understood the theorem, although in modern times it is incomprehensible to most. He said that although he is a rational scientist, he always bows down to great saints. He said that since childhood he has experienced God as being present everywhere.

Dr. Raghavacharyulu said that when he was a young man, his mother called him a "stupid fellow" and asked him why he didn't worship God (in a temple). "You show me a place where there is no God, then I will begin to worship!" he told her.

The scientists were led to Dr. Srivastava's puja room, where he meditates daily. He reverentially took from his altar a small Sri Yantra symbol, made of a copper-colored metal. But because it had been imbued with spiritual energies through sacred ritual, he only allowed them to look at it.

Dr. Srivastava said that he had been initiated by many saints and had practiced many methods of yoga. His meditation room contained pictures of great saints, including Paramahansa Yogananda (author of *Autobiography of a Yogi*), who the doctor

Paramahansa Yogananda, 1926
(Courtesy of Self-Realization Fellowship.)
Amma has great respect for this yogi saint. Paramahansa Yogananda was the first yogi to bring the spiritual science of Kriya Yoga to the West. His life story, first published in the United States in 1945, revealed the great spiritual heritage of India to millions of Western readers. His Autobiography of a Yogi *is part of a collection of spiritual books at the Amritapuri Ashram in India.*

said was one of his first teachers. He very matter-of-factly stated that the mystic amulet described in Yogananda's autobiography had the Sri Yantra symbol on it. He would not say how he knew this information.

According to the autobiography, one day a round silver amulet materialized in the hands of Yogananda's mother while she was praying. A holy man had previously come to her, telling her that this materialization would happen. He told her to make sure that the amulet be given to Yogananda, and said that his possession of it would awaken dormant memories in him to help with his spiritual mission on earth. The amulet was inscribed with Sanskrit mantras, or holy sounds—sounds, that when intoned properly, were spiritually beneficial.

It seemed very plausible that the Sri Yantra symbol was on the amulet. It is well known that Yogananda had great devotion to God as the Divine Mother. When he was a child, he worshipped Her in the statue form of Divine Mother Kali. But later in life Yogananda merged his consciousness with the primal sound of Aum, the formless aspect of the Goddess—which the Sri Yantra symbol represents.

Dr. Srivastava spoke about the difference between Eastern and Western science. India, he said, explores nature through the science of sound and consciousness. In India, spirituality itself is called a science—the knowledge of both the external "objective" world and internal "subjective" world. It is the science of knowing through personal experience—absolute truth—Brahman, or God.

In contrast, Western science explores nature through matter and light (electromagnetic energies).

Dr. Srivastava said, "If we limit science only to the 'objective' study of nature, then certainly we can reply only partially to body- and matter-related questions, and not at all to the mind and spiritually related questions."

Dr. D. N. Srivastava, Bhabha Atomic Research Centre

In his student days, Dr. Srivastava studied the life of the Indian saint Sri Chaitanya Mahaprabhu. He read the vivid descriptions of the flow of Divine Love from the saint's lips and face as he uttered the Holy Names of God. For many years, Dr. Srivastava had searched for someone with that much devotion.

He said, "I came across many saints, some of whom were really sincere in their pursuit, but none had that intensity of radiant bliss. But when I came in contact with Amma for the first time and heard her songs, I knew that I had found what I had been looking for for years. Just by sitting beside her I could feel the spiritual current that is experienced in deep meditation.

"Even in this age of hypocrisy, the number of dedicated seekers is not small. But complete dissolution in universal love, which Amma symbolizes, is an extremely rare phenomenon."

He proceeded to say they were learning how Amma was helping with the current world situation. He gave the following example: "Suppose there is a big lake of water that has been polluted. Then imagine that there are some philanthropic people who stand at the shoreline and start cleaning the water. At first only in their vicinity will the water be clean, but eventually that cleanliness will also reach all the remote corners of the lake.

"In a similar way, there is a mental atmosphere in our world that is being polluted by selfish desires. That also needs to be purified, but it cannot be purified by any mechanical gadget. The purification has to be accomplished by realized souls, by philanthropic work, by helping others, and by love. So whenever there is any soul like this, any saint—Amma is the best example—a purification starts to take place.

"There needs to be at least one high-level saint present in the world all the time. If there is no soul like Amma, the whole world will be in trouble. If there is no oxygen-replenishing mechanism in nature, such as plants, eventually the entire oxygen supply will get converted into carbon dioxide, and all life will vanish. In the same way, if there are no saints to clean this mental sphere by their spiritual practice, then the entire human race will perish."

Dr. Srivastava, trained as a physicist and in the spiritual science of India, said his life is dedicated to laying the foundations of a holistic system of knowledge in which the internal and external worlds are unified in such a way that there is no difference between them.

He said, "As such, nature doesn't differentiate between internal and external. These differentiations are a human invention that keeps the mind fragmented.

"Most people are fragmented personalities. And that fragmentation causes disharmony and chaos. If a person is not in harmony in his own being, how can he experience harmony in the world?"

Chapter 11

UNUSUAL SYNCHRONICITIES
Amma and the Dark-Faced Madonnas

C. G. Jung, the famous Swiss psychotherapist, knew from personal and professional experience that the Western psyche was greatly disturbed and fragmented, and that it suffered intensely from an overemphasis on rationalism. He felt that the "anima," or female aspect, was greatly suppressed within our psyche. Along with his patients, Jung had experienced the devastation of two world wars. During World War I, he felt that the outer battles he witnessed mirrored his own inner turmoil. Desperate to heal, Jung noticed sacred symbols spontaneously emerging in his dreams. Without knowing what they were, Jung began sketching these mandala images in his notebooks, and over a period of months he began to regain his sense of psychological wholeness.

Contiguous to Jung's exploration for wholeness, the divine feminine began manifesting as spiritual apparitions to poor but innocent children in different locations in war-torn Europe. The most famous and well documented of these apparitions happened on May 13, 1917, in the small, poor village of Fatima, Portugal. It was there that three illiterate children, Lucia, ten, and her cousins Jacinta, seven, and Francisco, nine, saw in a hillside

Russian Orthodox Church, Red Square, Moscow
(Courtesy of Louise Pare, 1997.)

Close-up of Madonna on Russian Orthodox Church

cove visions of a radiant lady dressed all in white. Because of their Christian upbringing, they perceived the lady to be the Holy Mother of God. The "Lady of Fatima" asked them to come on the thirteenth of each month for six months.

The Lady told Lucia to ask the pope and the bishops of the world to pray the rosary for world peace, and for the consecration of Russia to Her "Immaculate Heart." She told Lucia that Jesus wished to make use of her, to make the Lady of the Immaculate Heart acknowledged and loved throughout the world.

But the divine plea for formal consecration went unheeded for over fifty years.

Russia had converted to Byzantine Christianity in A.D. 988 and her people developed a great devotion to the Byzantine-inspired icons of the Madonna, the Mother of God. She was for them a Divine Mother of love, protection, and compassion.

But in 1917, Mother Russia was under the leadership of Lenin, who was influenced by Marxism. Marx, a rationalist and materialist, had no use for religion. He said it was the opiate of the people because he considered religion to be a blind belief that questioned nothing.

As a result, atheistic communism grew in power under the leadership of Lenin, Stalin, and other Soviet leaders. The people of Russia suffered religious, artistic, and political persecution, and many of the Russian churches were used as army barracks or museums. "Mother Russia" had become heartless. The divine feminine, its spiritual "heart," was trampled and desecrated.

In the meantime, C. G. Jung was deeply troubled by the destruction throughout Europe of the Christian churches and their religious symbols during the world wars. He felt that the role of religious symbols was to give sacred meaning to life, and that without them, humans would be at the mercy of the psychic "underworld." He left Europe and traveled to India to research sacred symbolism in religions worldwide.

It was in India that Jung first recognized that mandalas had ancient roots. In the East, he saw the mandala everywhere — the Hindu Sri Yantra (see page 67) and the Tibetan Buddhist mandalas. Jung learned that mandala symbolism in India was based on the yogic spiritual science of sound and consciousness, and that it represented wholeness, enlightenment, and psychological integration.

Jung intuited that atomic energy (matter) was somehow interconnected with the psyche (consciousness), but as a Western scientist, he was wary of taking up the Eastern spiritual science to investigate this relationship. Instead, he chose to explore the underlying reality that unified the psyche and atomic energy from the perspective of Western science, and he formed an alliance with the Nobel physicist Wolfgang Pauli.

Based on their work together, Jung coined the word *synchronicity* to define the unifying principle that connected psyche and matter. Synchronicity was for Jung an "acausal" principle connecting "objective" matter (atomic energy) and the psyche in a subjectively meaningful event or coincidence.

But Amma, like other great masters of India, told her monastics, "There is no such thing as matter; consciousness alone exists. If we approach all situations with this attitude, destruction becomes impossible for us; the very idea of destruction disappears. Only then can you help and serve others for their benefit and for the betterment of the world."

The great sages and yogis of India teach that when one is fully enlightened, one perceives the underlying unity of all reality as consciousness.

Sages and yogis have a highly developed spiritual intuition — that is, a direct perception of truth without any factual or sensory input—to know *all things*. They experience the whole cosmos as their Self. They know that all created things—atoms, liquids, gases, electricity, humans, plants, animals, bacteria, etc.—are but various forms of consciousness.

It is said that great sages and yogis can "foresee" the future.

Those who have been around Amma have witnessed many meaningful "synchronicities" and observed her uncanny ability to intuitively know when to act in the best interests of humanity. For example, in 1988, Amma told three Russians who visited her in Boston that she would be in Russia at an important time in their history. She made a statement about a future event that years later would come exactly true.

JANUARY 1991, SAN RAMON ASHRAM, CALIFORNIA

Staff members in California were preparing for Amma's fifth world tour to the United States and Europe when Amma sent word from India that the trip should include Russia. Meenakshi, a flight attendant for American Airlines, recalls standing in the vestibule of the ashram when the announcement was made.

"I always thought of Amma as the Virgin Mary," she said, "as the power of the Mother of God. Having been raised a Catholic, and having grown up as a teenager in the 1960s, I always thought of Russians as the bad guys. I remember the pope announcing, after Khrushchev's boast that he was going to bury us, that all the Catholics around the world should pray the rosary for world peace. So when I heard that Mother was going to Russia, I had this idea that she was going to transform everyone and open their hearts, and that this was what was foreseen years before by the pope."

Meenakshi thus perceived Amma's visit to Russia as a fulfillment of the prophecy of Our Lady of Fatima to bring peace to Russia.

·   ·   ·

On July 13, 1917, the Lady told the children that World War I would end, but if people did not stop offending God, a worse one would break out.

She told Lucia, "When you see a night illumined by an unknown light, know that this is the great sign given you by God that He is about to punish the world for its crimes, by means of war, famine, and persecutions of the Church, and of the Holy Father.

"To prevent this, I shall come to ask for the consecration of Russia to My Immaculate Heart and the communion of Reparation on the First Saturdays. If My requests are heeded, Russia will be converted, and there will be Peace; if not, she will spread her errors throughout the world, causing wars and persecutions of the Church. The good will be martyred, the Holy Father will have much to suffer, and various nations will be annihilated."

The Lady of Fatima went on to say, "In the end, My Immaculate Heart will triumph. The Holy Father will consecrate Russia to Me, and she will be converted. A period of peace will be granted to the world."

World War I did end, but on January 25, 1938, there was an unprecedented display of auroralike light seen throughout the European skies—even as far away as the United States—as was reported in newspapers worldwide. Forty-seven days later, Hitler annexed Austria, and the British and French, overawed by German rearmament, accepted his actions. Later that year, Hitler seized all of Czechoslovakia, and on September 1, 1939, he invaded Poland. World War II began on September 3, 1939, when Britain and France declared war on Germany in response to Hitler's invasion of Poland.

The Lady of Fatima had shown the children a vision of a fiery hell—what would result, she said, if her words were not taken seriously.

The children had been taught to think that God was in a heaven somewhere and that he would punish and send people to hell if they failed to stop offending him. They had no concept that humankind's mind-set and consequent actions create a karmic result if cosmic laws are broken. From an Eastern perspective, hell (holocaust) is created by the overrational and fragmented human psyche.

Looking back over the events of the past hundred years (1900–1999), the truth of this perspective becomes very clear.

A fiery, human-made hell happened in August 1945, when the world's first atom bombs were dropped on the Japanese cities of Hiroshima and Nagasaki by the United States. The glaring pink light in the sky burned peoples' eyes out, and anyone within a mile of the explosions was incinerated. Approximately 250,000 people were killed. World War II was over, but it had claimed forty million lives and left in its burning embers two world powers—Russia and the United States.

In 1917, Our Lady of Fatima also revealed to Lucia what has become known as the third part of the Fatima secret, which has never been revealed to the public. Lucia asked the pope to reveal it no later than 1960, but that was never done.

Pope John XXIII suppressed the secret, as did his successors.

In 1962, the Vatican-Moscow Agreement took place in secret at Metz, France. It has been postulated that the Vatican, in order to assure that observers of the Russian Orthodox Church could attend the Second Vatican Council, made an agreement with Moscow that the Council would contain no explicit condemnation of communism.

On the anniversary of Our Lady of Fatima's first appearance, May 13, 1981, Pope John Paul II rode smiling and waving in an open car through excited throngs of pilgrims in St. Peter's Square. A young Turk named Mehmet Ali Agca fired two shots at close range in an attempt to assassinate the pope. One shot hit the pope's abdomen, barely missing vital organs. Pope John Paul felt deeply that the Lady of Fatima had saved his life.

It is interesting to note that in Medjugorje, Yugoslavia, from March 1, 1984, to January 8, 1987, another apparition of the divine feminine appeared to six children. Known as the Queen of Peace, she told the children that there is only one God. She said she was the "Mother" of everyone and that her children must respect all faiths. All religions are equal before God, she said, and in God there are no divisions. Only hatred creates division. She told them to act with love in the place where they lived.

On March 25, 1984, fifty-five years after the Fatima apparitions, Pope John Paul II made a formal consecration of the world to the Immaculate Heart of Mary, in St. Peter's Square.

The next year, in 1985, Mikhail Gorbachev came into power.

By 1990, Gorbachev had instigated many reforms, including cutting back on nuclear armaments and the use of force to prevent the democratic transformation of Russian satellite states, which was instrumental in the fall of the Berlin Wall. For his peace initiatives and democratization policies, he was awarded the Nobel Peace Prize. But there was still much social unrest in the country, and many hard-line Communists opposed him and his reforms.

AMMA'S WORLD TOUR, 1991

Russia was the last destination on the tour that year. At the last minute, Amma changed her scheduled time of arrival to Russia, even though all the airline tickets had already been bought. She had her staff reschedule the date of her arrival to August 17.

On Amma's first morning program in Moscow, only about fifty or seventy-five people came to receive her blessings, since no formal notices had been posted. People had heard about her only through the spiritual underground. There was a little book table set up in the small concrete hall to sell Amma's Indian biography, translated into Russian, and some other religious objects. But when the Holy Mother started giving darshan and realized how poor the people were, she gave everything away for free.

Moscow was very depressed, and food was scarce or nonexistent. Ramana, who was born in America, was one of the monastics who had traveled to Russia with Amma. He couldn't help but notice the sad state of affairs. "The shops were empty. All that you could see for sale were walnuts and watermelons. Everywhere walnuts and watermelons. Anytime there was anything good, you would see a huge line going around the block. That would mean somebody had something worth selling."

The next morning, August 19, three hundred people came to the program. They were crying and visibly afraid. They told Amma that the government was very unstable, and they didn't know what was going to happen next. While Amma was listening to their concerns, tanks started rolling in the streets toward Red Square. Men arrived carrying guns, and roads were barricaded.

During the darshan, Amma was informed that Gorbachev had been put under house arrest. He carried with him his briefcase, which contained all of the secret nuclear information on weapons and warheads.

Amma canceled the afternoon, evening, and next day's programs. She and some of the monastics went back to the apartment where she was staying and watched the politicians on TV.

Elena, a Russian devotee, had accompanied Amma despite the emotional difficulty of doing so. She felt anger toward her parents, who lived in Leningrad. Sixteen years earlier, she had left Russia because she detested the atrocities inflicted by the government on her friends. She recalls Amma's support during this troublesome time: "The inexhaustible power of Mother's love enabled me to overcome my resistance to seeing my parents again, something I did not want to do. But then, Mother's love miraculously resulted in their traveling with me from their home in Leningrad to Moscow to meet her. At the program, something happened that initially made me uncomfortable, but happily resulted in my father and Amma becoming instant friends.

"My father was having a hard time relaxing and decided that before the evening program, he would have a drink. Shortly after that, uninhibited and happy, he arrived at the hall. Though his behavior was okay, his breath gave him away. I was mortified and judgmental. But Mother was loving and accepting, laughing and calling him her 'big baby.' She won his heart.

"I will always have a picture in my mind of my father throwing her kisses and repeating in Russian, *Chto za zhenschina!* (What a woman!)"

Now came the problem of how to get Amma and everyone else safely out of the country on August 20, as scheduled. Amma's personal assistant, Swamini Amritaprana, recalls, "Even on the way to the airport, we didn't know if we were going to make it there. There were tanks everywhere. In the end, we made it, but it was quite something to be in that country at such a crucial time."

Elena said, "In my view, it was no accident that Mother's first trip to Russia occurred during three of the most eventful days in the history of the world. Her coming, I believe, symbolized the opening and healing of Russia. Just as she sucked the pus out of the leper in Kerala, so did her presence in Russia allow people to cleanse their hearts, believe in themselves, and stand up for the truth."

After the abortive coup by the Communist hard-liners in August 1991, a huge Orthodox Christian congregation, numbering in the hundreds of thousands, gathered in Red Square in Moscow, to the backdrop of a Russian Orthodox church containing icons of the Dark-Faced Madonna (see illustration on page 162) to praise God and celebrate a mass of thanksgiving to the Lord for the victory of freedom and democracy they had won.

In July 1992, Amma took a second trip to Russia. She gave a speech, translated through Renata, a Russian translator: "I am not just a Hindu woman, coming to Russia, trying to convert you to another religion. I come in a difficult moment of Russian history to give people hope for the future. In the past, Russia needed czars, force, and rigid structure. The country was ruled by the masculine, and now it is time to be influenced by the feminine.

"We do not know each other's language, and yet we are like two banks of the same river. The river is God's love, which unites both sides of the river. Mother hopes that her love will unite both sides, which seem so independent of each other."

Amma told the people who came to her public program that Gorbachev's reforms had opened the gate to freedom. Amma told the Russian people, "However, freedom means responsibility—responsibility to yourself, to others, and to God. We must understand that life is led by God and not only by ourselves. Responsibility and love go hand in hand. Without love, it is impossible to live."

Amma encouraged the people to have a cheerful and positive attitude and to be more kind. "Without spiritual growth, you cannot have material abundance or enjoy any material well-being. Once the seed is planted, it will take time to grow. We must take care and be patient."

. . .

Throughout all of Europe, there are strong ritual traditions for venerating the Dark-Faced Mother, to whom generations of people have ascribed miraculous healing powers. Multicultural images of her abound throughout France, Italy, Spain, England, Belgium, Austria, Germany, Switzerland, Poland, and various other countries in Europe.

During the years when the Solidarity movement was banned in Poland by the Communist government there, Solidarity leader Lech Walesa always wore a picture of the famous Black Madonna of Czestochowa on his lapel.

The Dark Mother is known by different names. Catholics call her the Black Madonna, the Buddhists call her Tara, and the Gypsies, who migrated to Europe from India, have called her by the name of Sara/Kali. And there are the ancient Dark Mothers: Sophia from the Old Testament, Artemis of Ephesus, the Roman Ceres, and Isis the Egyptian goddess. In fact, the Dark Mother is venerated in some form all over the world.

The Dark Mother has been a powerful icon for those who seek to balance spiritual ignorance with compassion and love. Her role is protector of the poor and oppressed.

Amma has visited many European countries, bringing her healing balm of love and compassion to all who are open to receiving it. That the dark-faced female sage from Kerala, India, should attract a large following in Europe should come as no surprise. Many of Amma's followers experience her as the "Mother of Love and Compassion"—qualities attributed to the Dark Mother, which is so deeply etched in the European psyche.

In Kerala, thousands of Indians believe Amma is an incarnation of Divine Mother Kali. Many of the Indian swamis who have been around her for any length of time have experienced what they call Amma's "dark Kali nature." Although she is loving and compassionate, they have found that she does not hesitate to scold them when she feels it is necessary to uproot their egotistical tendencies.

Many people may think that the Dark Mother is manifest only within Amma, other Hindu mystics, or is somehow contained within the statues and icons that many Europeans have externally worshipped for centuries. However, the Hindu sages teach that "Mother" is within each of us as creative Shakti energy—in fact there is no place she is not.

According to Jungian therapists Marion Woodman and Elinor Dickson, many of their Western patients tell of having potent dreams of the Dark Mother.

Marion and Elinor said, "Today her darkness is associated with the unknown, repressed side of our femininity. Experiencing her in our body is a starting step toward experiencing ourselves whole. That sense of wholeness is essential to healing.

"So long as we deny the Great Mother and refuse to integrate her as Goddess in our psychic development, we will continue to act out neurotic fantasies and endanger our very survival as a species."

The following story illustrates how experiencing the Mother within the body leads to experiencing oneself as whole.

THE HEALING POWER OF THE BLACK MADONNA

Father Bede Griffiths (1906–1993), born in England and educated at Oxford, became a Catholic Benedictine monk at the Prinknask Priory in Gloucestershire. However in 1955, at age forty-nine, he left the monastery and traveled to Kerala, in southern India, in search of the "other half of his soul"—the feminine intuitive dimension. He felt that his monastic training and the whole Western approach to God had left out the feminine.

Amma was just a child of two when Father Bede arrived in India. According to Judy Walter, an American nurse and long-time friend, Bede first became aware of Amma only in 1991, as a result of foreign visitors to his ashram located in Tamil Nadu.

Bede's intention in going to India was not to convert the Hindus to Christianity. At his ashram, Bede integrated both Hindu and Christian rituals because he wanted East and West to learn from each other at the deepest possible level.

Although he never met Amma, in the early 1980s, without knowing anything about her life or mystical experiences, he started having a strong desire to have an inner experience of the Divine Mother. This desire was stimulated in part by his extensive reading of Hindu scriptures. In his sermons and writings he spoke of the Divine Mother in Hindu terms of the Shakti energy—the feminine power of the divine that is rooted within each person.

On January 25, 1990, several months after Bede's book *The New Vision of Reality* was published, he had what doctors termed a slight stroke, and congestive heart failure. But for Bede it was nothing less than a profound transformative experience of the Divine Mother (Shakti energy) rising up within him as the power of the Black Madonna.

Bede said, "The Black Madonna symbolized for me the black power in nature and life. The hidden power in the womb. I feel it was this power that struck me." He found her power to be paradoxically cruel and destructive but at the same time deeply loving, nourishing, and protecting.

He said, "I felt the need to surrender to the Mother, and very soon it became clear to me that it was not only Mother Mary but also Mother Nature, Mother Earth, my own mother, motherhood itself."

The experience of the Black Madonna power had altered

Bede's perception in a radical way. "It blew down barriers, and I no longer saw things in neat categories. I felt like my ego had collapsed, and I felt totally free. When I wrote the book *The New Vision of Reality* it came from my head. But now I really understand with my whole being this new vision of reality.

"The sense that I was healed was very strong. Psychologically, I think it meant that the feminine had recovered. The cure I felt was a deep surge of feminine love—it was this sense that I was loved that made me weep. More and more I feel the union of the masculine and the feminine in myself, and this has come out strikingly in my theological understanding of this experience."

Exactly one month after his stroke, he experienced a tremendous pressure in his head and was convinced he was dying. Although he was quite prepared to die, he had a sudden intuition to surrender to the "Mother." "I somehow made a surrender to the Mother. Then I had an experience of overwhelming love. Waves of love sort of flowed into me. Judy Walter, my great friend, was watching. I called out to her, 'I'm being overwhelmed by love.' "

Father Bede said he grew more in the two years after his stroke than in the previous eighty-four. He lived for three more years. During this period, it was strikingly obvious, to Judy and to all of his friends, how this experience transformed him. She said, "This very reserved, proper Englishman became warmer and freer in all his relationships. It was as if the emotional fountain at the core of his being began to flow over with life-giving waters. He could be moved to tears and was not afraid to cry with or for others."

A huge surge of interest in the divine feminine was rallied in December 1996, when the Catholic and Christian Orthodox churches made a concerted ecumenical effort to honor Mary the Mother of God. It was at that time that Pope John Paul II and Bartholomew, patriarch of Constantinople, each blessed hundreds of Black Madonna icons along with various other representations of the Mother of God. For three years, these images of the divine feminine traveled all over Europe and to different parts of the world.

In 1997, one of the places scheduled to receive one of the traveling Black Madonna icons was Estella, Spain, a place Amma was scheduled to go that summer.

Christina Jencks, an American woman who traveled all over Europe with Amma that summer, said, "We drove twenty-four hours from Assisi, Italy, to Estella, Spain, where Amma was to give her programs for the first time. The town is near the city of Pamplona, where they have the bullfights and run the bulls through the streets every year. When we arrived, the bull running was just over. Traditionally, the Spanish people wear white with red scarves on that day.

"So, when we arrived, Amma's swamis, not knowing this tradition, thought all these people were coming to Mother's program [devotees of Amma dress in white]. Red and white are the colors of the Divine Mother. It was interesting to me that the day Mother arrived, everyone was walking around in red and white.

"We drove to the edge of town and immediately went three-quarters of the way up a hill to a very small monastery. That's where Mother stayed during the two and a half days she was in Estella. Attached to the monastery, there was a very small old church.

"After arriving, Mother went into the church, looked around, smiled, nodded her head, and said, 'Meditate here.' So, many of the women who were on the tour would go there every morning to meditate in its very beautiful, concentrated energy.

"On the altar, in the center of the room, a three- or four-foot-high, brightly silver-colored icon of the Divine Mother, holding the baby Jesus, was seated in a crescent moon. Installed just slightly lower than the silver Madonna was a Black Madonna, with a huge bouquet of flowers beneath it. White candles burned

Notre Dame Du Puy
(Courtesy of Francis Ramé, 1997.)
*This traveling Black Madonna icon was enshrined in the monastery
chapel in Estella during the time Amma was there.*

brightly on either side of it, setting off the blackness of the Madonna's face in a very beautiful and powerful way.

"The church was circular, with curved, stained-glass windows and wooden pews. Names of adoration to Mother Mary were written in each section of the stained glass as part of the design: 'To the Mother Mary who is the most beautiful,' 'To the Mother who is the most compassionate,' 'To the Mother who knows everyone's heart.' It reminded me of the one hundred and eight names of the Divine Mother that we chant in honor of Amma."

Francis Ramé, the driver for the Holy Mother's van to Estella, Spain, was startled to see the traveling relic of the Black Madonna sitting on the altar. He recognized it as the Notre Dame Du Puy from his small village of Baillet-en-France. Francis later found out, to his amazement, that Christian organizers from the local church in Estella had specifically asked for the Notre Dame Du Puy to come to their town. Just a day or two before Amma arrived, the traveling Black Madonna relic was installed on the altar. And it was taken from the chapel the very day she left.

The silver Madonna permanently installed in the chapel has a remarkable history. It was found in a cave near the top of the mountain in 1085 by some shepherds. Its location was revealed to them in an apparition. Nobody knew how it got there. The shepherds went to the king of Spain and asked him what to do with this relic that they had found. He said, "Take it to one of the churches and install it there." But when they tried to remove it from the mountain, it grew heavier and heavier and heavier, making it impossible for the shepherds to transport it down the mountain.

The shepherds went back to the king and told him what had happened. He told them to let the Mother stay where she wanted, and to build the church around her. Thus the church connected to the monastery where Amma stayed was built to install this holy icon near its original site.

Estella was a most challenging place to get to. Amma and her monastics had to take two planes and fly through Barcelona to Bilbao, and then drive for an hour. After the 1997 visit to Estella, a lot of the local people suggested to the Holy Mother that she should go to Madrid or Barcelona, because they were the biggest cities.

The monastics too wanted to go to a large city, for the sake of convenience, and because it would be less grueling on Amma. But Amma insisted that they return to Estella.

In January 1999, Swamini Amritaprana learned for the first time that there had been years and years of fighting in the Basque region near Estella, and many people had been killed.

The Basque people have had to fight to guard their centuries-old culture. The most brutal reminder of past repression and ethnic purgation is found close to Estella, in the Basque town of Guernica. During the 1937 Spanish civil war, the Spanish dictator had allowed Germany to bomb the town, so as to teach the independent-minded Basques a lesson. The Spanish artist Pablo Picasso painted his famous *Guernica* as an act of political protest against this act of violence.

After Amma left Estella in 1998, a peace treaty was signed in the Basque region.

Swamini Amritaprana said, "The Spanish people from the area find it so synchronous that the peace treaty was signed after Amma went there. They really feel it was Amma's grace and presence that finally brought peace to this region."

As of this writing, the peace treaty lasted for one and a half years.

On May 13, 2000, the anniversary of Our Lady of Fatima's appearance, the pope disclosed the Third Secret of Fatima. Originally intended to be published in 1960, it has been the subject of great controversy, causing numerous speculations ranging from worldwide nuclear annihilation to deep rifts in the Roman Catholic Church.

However, Cardinal Angelo Sodano, the Vatican secretary of state, insisted that the Third Secret was no "doomsday prophecy." According to the Associated Press, Cardinal Sodano explained that the once concealed part of the prophecies said to have been revealed to three Portuguese shepherd children by an apparition of the Virgin Mary in 1917 was a vision of an attempt to kill a pope.

Because the Third Secret had been withheld for so long, a number of people believed that publishing a photocopy of the original was the only way to ensure that the document was authentic. In June 2000, a forty-page, interpretive pamphlet of the Third Secret was released by the Vatican. But Father Kramer of the Fatima Center described the Vatican's interpretation as a "whitewash."

Father Kramer said, "First, in his announcement at Fatima, Sodano himself admits that the actual text of the secret 'contains a prophetic vision similar to those found in Sacred Scripture,' involving 'events spread out over time in a succession and duration which are not specified.' Yet in the same statement he said that events mentioned in the Third Secret now 'seem part of the past.' Which is it—events of a duration not specified or events in the past?

"And, if the events in the Third Secret 'now seem part of the past,' why do we need this commentary in the first place? Does Our Lady speak in riddles, so that we need commentators to translate Her words describing things which have supposedly already happened?"

Chapter 12

THE MIRACLE OF AIMS
Heart-Centered Medicine

Dr. Prem Nair had all the wealth and success that he had ever wanted. He had all the luxuries that most Americans yearn for—professional status, expensive cars, a large attractive, landscaped home with a pool, and a lovely devoted wife, Radhika, and two intelligent children—a daughter, Priya, and a son, Krishnanunni.

He and his wife were raised in wealthy families in Mumbai, India. After finishing medical school, he moved to the United States and earned a postgraduate degree in medicine at the University of Southern California in Los Angeles, where he specialized in internal medicine, gastroenterology, and liver diseases. Dr. Nair had developed a lucrative private practice, and was also a professor of medicine at the University of Southern California College of Medicine, where he directed the Gastroenterology Program at the Hospital of the Good Samaritan in Los Angeles.

He was brought up a Hindu by his father, who was a deeply spiritual man, and a devotee of the great nineteenth-century Indian saint Ramakrishna Paramahansa (see the illustration on page 60). Ramakrishna had a deep devotion to God as Divine Mother and meditated constantly on her in the form of a statue of Kali at the Dakshineswar Temple near Calcutta. But just praying to her in the form of a statue was not enough. He had an intense agonizing yearning to have an authentic vision of Divine Mother, like the visions she gave to other Hindu mystics. Ramakrishna said, "Greatly afflicted with the thought that I might never have Mother's vision, I was in great agony. I thought that there was no use in living such a life. My eyes suddenly fell upon the sword that was there in the Mother's [Kali] temple. I made up my mind to put an end to my life with it that very moment. Like a madman I ran and caught hold of it, when suddenly I had a wonderful vision of the Mother, and fell down unconscious.

"I did not know what happened then in the external world. But, in my heart of hearts, there was flowing a current of intense bliss, never experienced before, and I had the immediate knowledge of the Light that is Mother. It was as if the houses, doors, temples, and all other things vanished altogether; as if there was nothing anywhere! And what I saw was a boundless infinite Conscious Sea of Light!"

Unlike his father, Dr. Nair was not in the least interested in spirituality. Career and material gain were his focus—that is, until he met Amma.

One day in 1989, Dr. Nair's brother telephoned him from India to tell him he had a problem with his neck, and that the physicians he had consulted could do nothing to help him. Dr. Nair suggested his brother come to the United States to be treated.

But his brother said there was no need for him to come to the United States because he would be taken care of by a woman named Amma, who was a saint. Dr. Nair asked his brother what on earth her being a saint had to do with his neck problem.

His brother told him, "Ramakrishna worshipped Kali in the form of a statue. And now Kali has come to us in a living form."

These words triggered a dramatic physical and psychological change in Dr. Nair. "When my brother said this, something very

strange happened to me. It was as if some molecular rearrange-
ment took place and my whole being was transformed in less than
a moment."

As soon as Dr. Nair put the phone down, he booked a flight to
India. During his five years in private practice he had never
taken a day off, and now to the astonishment of his wife, as he
recalls, "I left without even telephoning my office to say that I
wouldn't be in the next day. I had no idea what I was doing. My
whole being was focused on the thought of Amma."

Dazed and jet-lagged, Dr. Nair arrived at Amma's Amritapuri
Ashram carrying only a small bag slung over his shoulder. The
first person he saw was Swami Amritaswarupananda, who asked
him where he had come from. He told the swami he had never
met Amma, but that it was important for him to see her.

Swami told Dr. Nair Amma's life story, and the swami was so
moved when he spoke that tears streamed down his face. Then
he led Dr. Nair to the darshan hut. Entering the hut, Dr. Nair
saw Amma's radiant and smiling face for the first time. He was
directed to sit on the floor with a number of other devotees who
were also waiting to receive her darshan. The energy of her love
and compassion was palpable even before he went up to her.

Dr. Nair's turn came to receive her hug. In her arms, he felt he
was being reunited with someone he had deeply loved and spiritually revered in some ancient past. He wanted to stay in India
and be with her for some time. But Amma told him that she
would see him in America.

So the next day, Dr. Nair flew back to California to face a
bewildered wife who was furious at his strange and sudden
absence. He arrived home with armfuls of books and cassette
tapes that he had brought from the ashram.

To help his wife understand his new devotion and attraction to
Amma, he put on one of the cassettes of her singing *bhajans*. "My

wife, who, like me, had never in her life been even remotely interested in anything spiritual, was mesmerized by the songs and by
Amma's voice. She suddenly broke down in a torrent of tears, and
in that moment she was transformed as rapidly as I had been."

From that day onward, Dr. Nair and his wife, who had led very
materialistic lives, were changed people. Everything that had
interested them before suddenly seemed trivial. Shortly afterward, Radhika flew with their children to India to live in an austere room at Amma's ashram.

In his newfound spirituality and devotion, Dr. Prem Nair began
asking Amma's advice in all matters, including his physical health.
One day, he discovered a large, rock-hard lump in his groin. He
was diagnosed with lymphoma, and the doctors told him that he
would need to have an operation and a bone-marrow transplant.

He telephoned Amma in Germany, where she was on her
world tour. On the phone she consoled Prem and told him not
to worry, and to go ahead with the operation. Ron Gottsegen, a
close disciple, was with Amma at the time Dr. Nair called. Ron
said when Amma got off the phone she had tears flowing from
her eyes and told him that Prem had cancer. In the meantime,
Dr. Nair went ahead with the surgery, and made preparations for
a bone-marrow transplant.

But after surgery, he and the doctors discovered that all the
lymph nodes, which had grown to massive sizes, were completely
free of tumors. The doctors told Dr. Nair that they were astonished because that type of growth was usually a clear sign of lymphoma. And in subsequent tests, no evidence was ever found of
the disease.

Dr. Nair felt it was Amma's grace that had cured him. Shortly
after his surgery, he flew to Europe to be with Amma on her world
tour. After he had spent two weeks with her, she gently suggested
that he go back to United States and resume his medical practice.

Like many people who have been inspired by Amma's vision to serve God in the poor and suffering, Dr. Nair gave up all his worldly possessions, and in 1994 he moved to the Amritapuri Ashram to live a spiritual life, devoid of material comforts. He began selflessly serving in Amma's charities, just as his wife and children were doing.

In the early 1990s, Amma told her monastics that she had a vision of creating a very specialized hospital that would offer the most modern medical care to the poor and destitute. In her travels throughout India, she became aware that thousands of adults and children suffered from heart problems. They were on long waiting lists of four to seven years and would probably never get treatment.

Her young monastics were perplexed by her vision. They were not particularly interested in the physical body and its needs, as their whole focus was on realizing their divinity. Besides, the ashram had no money or land, and no one with expertise in construction. Swamini Amritaprana voiced the concerns of a number of other monastics. "To be honest, when I first heard Amma suggesting the plan for a hospital, I thought, 'How on earth is such an enormous project going to take place? Who will finance it, supervise construction, and take care of the thousands of details? And who will run it?' "

Amma told them that the Hindu scriptures say that it is important to sustain the body. She asked them to examine the history of great Indian saints like Sri Ramakrishna, Ramana Maharshi, and Swami Vivekananda, because they all underwent medical treatments when they fell ill.

"It is the nature of the body to become sick," she said. "Therefore, it's important to undergo required medical treatment. In order to know God, it is necessary to preserve the physical instrument—the body. Therefore, hospitals and treatment are not incompatible with spirituality. They are crucial in maintaining the body, which is a means to know the soul [Self]."

The scriptures say that sages have only to think of something for it to happen. It was Amma's vision, determined will, and focused creative energy that made the Amrita Institute of Medical Sciences (AIMS) Hospital possible.

Amma insisted that the hospital be built in the shape of a six-petaled lotus, and she entrusted the responsibility of the construction of the hospital to Brahmachari Divyamrita, who started the project with nothing more than his unswerving faith in Amma.

Before coming to Amma's ashram in 1979, Divyamrita's only professional "expertise" was in running a small bakery from his home. He made sweets and bread, which he then distributed by bicycle to the bakeries in his town. When Divyamrita first came to the ashram, he had just had a heart valve replacement operation. Amma had showered him with love and attention.

Swami Amritaswarupananda has been with Amma since 1978 and has witnessed many times how she takes "ordinary" people like Brahmachari Divyamrita and completely transforms them through the power of her love.

"I cannot believe how Amma made an expert out of this boy," the swami said. "It is unbelievable. He doesn't have any skills, in the sense that he doesn't have an engineering degree. He has only an eighth-grade education. In those early days I wondered, 'Why is Mother giving so much importance to this person? Why is she spending so much time showering him with love, attention, and compassion, in order to make a better person out of him?'

"I thought—'Look at this boy! He is physically weak. He cannot do any hard work. He has just had a very serious operation. How can he function in the world outside the ashram?' And I looked at his mind, which was so unhealthy. When I recall this boy's earlier nature, and compare it with his current responsibilities, I am amazed."

Divyamrita is presently in charge of supervising the construction of the twenty-five thousand free homes for the homeless, the engineering college, and Amma's many schools throughout India, plus the maintenance of all the hundred or more ashram vehicles.

Divyamrita was put in charge of supervising all the details of the construction of the AIMS project. Toward the end of 1992, Brahmachari Divyamrita found a location for the proposed hospital near Eddapally, three kilometers from Cochin.

The site they chose consisted of twenty-two acres—one acre of land and twenty-one acres of water, five to six feet deep. It was owned by thirty-seven people, all of whom had to be separately negotiated with as part of the sale.

Private contractors presented the devotees with huge estimates for landfill, pointing out that it would be a tremendous task to convert the swampland into a usable site for a hospital. At this juncture, Amma asked Divyamrita not to seek the help of outside contractors but to proceed with the work himself.

Undaunted, Brahmachari Divyamrita mobilized assistant "laborers" for the construction of the hospital. His workforce consisted of unskilled men and women monastics and devotees. A four-acre hillside, ten kilometers away from the site, was purchased for its soil. Some monastics were assigned the task of digging soil from the hillside, while others remained at the site to unload the trucks of fresh dirt.

Swami Amritaswarupananda was awed at Amma's foresight. "Now I know why God is known as the Creator! Because I have seen, and have experienced, how Amma is creating a spiritual empire around her. Mother knew that Divyamrita was the instrument to do all these things. Mother always says, 'I want ordinary people, because they will have the love, the sincerity, the right attitude, the heart, and they will have the faith. If they are too intellectual, they can only question and doubt. And in doubting and questioning, you lose so much energy. But with faith, you have tremendous power and energy to do the work.' "

It has been said that great masters give their disciples certain duties, not because the disciple would be good for the work, but rather because the work would be good for the disciple.

Ron Gottsegen, administrative director of the AIMS Hospital, tells the following story to illustrate this point. "The person who was vital to setting up the whole computer system for the hospital was asked by Amma to go back to the ashram. I and others felt that this person's leaving was a great loss to the projects getting done on time.

"However this person's need to be at the ashram was far more important than Amma's hospital. It showed her respect for that individual. And of course the project didn't stop. Other people rose to the occasion, as always happens. I only say this by way of explanation that Amma's primary concern is not with the hospital. It's with each and every one of her children's spiritual growth."

When Dr. Prem Nair first went to live in India, he had heard of Amma's plans to build a hospital, but he had thought that it would be another charitable hospital, like so many he had seen in India, that provide low-cost treatment and have only low-technology care. He thought Amma's hospital would require only a minimum of his time.

Little did Dr. Prem know what was in store for him.

"I arrived at the hospital site on a bright, sunny day to find that

Brahmachari Divyamrita

the backwater site was slowly and laboriously being filled with mud brought from the nearby hillside. At the time there was only a handful of people at the project site and several trucks dumping mud, followed by compaction. This continued for many months. Subsequently, piling began with huge drills on tripods. It seemed like an endless task. Over the next year, the piling work progressed slowly and painfully. On careful scrutiny, the work being done was truly phenomenal. Massive, thirty-meter-deep holes were being drilled into the ground, into which fabricated steel columns were placed. Enormous amounts of cement were then poured into the steel columns to support a structure that I could not imagine at the time."

Amma entrusted Dr. Nair with the job of making the first blueprints for the proposed 800-bed, state-of-the-art hospital.

Working from his vast medical experience, he collaborated with a team of hospital architects to lay out the space for the various medical specialties, and to integrate it into a physical building with six towers representing the petals of a lotus, as Amma had envisioned it to be.

It was a very difficult challenge, and the architects at first strongly resisted it. However, everyone discovered after the hospital was complete that it was an excellent model. It afforded them the ability to do many things that they would not have been able to do if they had gone with a conventional Western model.

When asked about the meaning of the lotus shape of the hospital, Amma said, "In India, the lotus flower is a symbol of purity, perfection, and bliss. We visualize our gods and goddesses seated on lotuses. The lotus is the greatest among flowers. We call the heart a lotus. It makes us happy just to see a blossoming flower. The lotuslike structure of the AIMS Hospital symbolizes the principles of peace, well-being, and happiness.

"Also, it is a reminder that we do our spiritual practices so that the flower of our hearts will blossom. Rather than simply calling our hearts 'flowers,' we should try to become like flowers, so that we can spread our perfume and beauty throughout the world."

. . .

On May 23, 1994, Amma laid the foundation stone of the hospital.

Around this time, Ron Gottsegen, a successful American businessman, was asked by Amma and Swami Amritaswarupananda to help Dr. Nair on the project. He first met Amma in 1987 and since then had been a devotee. At her request, he moved to Cochin, India, in 1997 and became the administrative executive of the hospital. He had sold his electronics company and, shortly after meeting Amma in 1987, has dedicated his whole life to selfless service.

According to Ron, it has cost about twenty-five million dollars to build and equip AIMS for its current level of operation. He said, "The financing has been accomplished through the generosity of the devotees and people worldwide who have been inspired by Amma's own example. They have donated money, equipment, and time, and it is strictly from these donations that the facility has been built and is functioning. Currently the estimated monthly costs for running AIMS is one million dollars."

Ron Gottsegen said that not all professionals who work at AIMS get paid, but instead, they donate their services out of a motivation to serve the poor. AIMS was officially dedicated to the service of humanity on May 17, 1998. Within a year and a half of opening its doors, 115,000 outpatients and 11,000 inpatients have been served, including over 4,500 children with heart defects. The hospital provides the highest quality of medical care to all patients regardless of race, religion, caste, or ability to pay. But those who can pay, do pay—according to their ability, but at substantially reduced levels from the commercial hospitals.

In addition to medical and surgical heart treatments, the hospital provides specialty care for those who suffer from all types of kidney, digestive, and pulmonary diseases.

The hospital gives forth a sense of beauty and peace. Every door, window frame, wooden-sculpted stair railing, and most of

Ron Gottsegen and Dr. Prem Nair, Cochin, India

the furniture was thoughtfully handcrafted at the site by skilled and "unskilled" laborers willing to learn new skills under the supervision of Brahmachari Rajeev. Visitors and patients have described AIMS as a feeling of being in a holy temple—a vibration of love permeates the atmosphere.

All destitute patients who come to the hospital are greeted with reverence and loving concern—even former enemies of Amma. She tells her spiritual seekers, "Children, real love and devotion to God is to be compassionate toward the poor and suffering. Feed those who are hungry, help the destitute, console those who grieve, and give relief to the suffering."

Amrita Institute of Medical Sciences, Cochin, India
*This hospital, built with love and devotion, serves the poor and suffering
with state-of-the-art medical equipment and staff. In March 2000, surgeons
and nurses from Boston's Children's Hospital, the University of Chicago,
and the University of Minnesota have visited AIMS to share their expertise.*

One man who benefited greatly from heart surgery at the new
AIMS Hospital was originally a great antagonist of Amma's. The
man, a fisherman, was part of a family of twenty-four children
who lived in Amma's village.

In the late 1970s, his whole family, including his uncles and
cousins, greatly opposed Amma and her family. At that time, he
was a rationalist and a hard-core Communist. One evening after

Prime Minister of India, Bramachari Shubamrita, and Amma at AIMS Inaugeration
On May 17, 1998, the prime minister of India, Mr. A. B. Vajpayee, helped inaugurate the AIMS Hospital and lauded Amma for the example of selfless service that she is setting for the Indian nation and the world.

Amma finished Devi Bhava, he tried to injure Acchan by hitting him brutally on the back, knocking him down.

Twenty years later, in early 1999, the man discovered that he had a serious heart problem. Being poor, he went to the ashram to see if he could get free treatment at the new hospital. Because he had tried to injure Acchan, the monastics told the man that he must first obtain a letter of permission from Acchan.

Acchan not only forgave the man, but he also gave him a letter of permission so that he could have free surgery—an expensive heart surgery that would normally cost 300,000 Indian rupees, or about eight thousand dollars—an impossible sum for a poor Indian.

After the operation, the man could not work at all. So every month, Amma gave him some money to cover his expenses. Neither she nor Acchan expected anything back in return.

In addition to the monumental accomplishment of AIMS, Amma's arms of compassion for the sick have embraced the building of Amrita Kripa Sagar, a hospice near Mumbai for terminally ill cancer patients, and Amrita Kripa, a charitable hospital located at the Amritapuri Ashram that provides free medical care to the villagers and thousands of visiting devotees. Her devotees also run free medical dispensaries in most of her ashram centers all over India, and on the horizon is a vision for a hospital specifically for AIDS patients.

Chapter 13

QUALITIES OF A TRUE
SPIRITUAL MASTER
HEALING THE DEEPEST OF SPIRITUAL WOUNDS

On May 15, 1987, the Amritapuri Ashram was plunged into a state of deep sadness. That day marked the beginning of Amma's first world tour to Singapore, the United States, and Europe. The Indian brahmacharis and brahmacharinis who accompanied her to the Trivandrum airport had tears in their eyes to see her leave.

Just before walking into the building, Amma touched her folded hands to her forehead and bowed to her children, saying, "It is for the benefit of all the crying souls out there that Amma is traveling. Those who live in other countries are also Amma's children. It is to soothe their pain, to alleviate their sorrow, and to show them the eternal light that Amma is going abroad."

Since that first world tour twelve years ago, Amma has alleviated the sorrows and soothed the pain of many Westerners. A number of the Westerners who she healed had suffered from betrayal by spiritual leaders who abused them financially, sexually, or emotionally.

Spiritual betrayal is one of the deepest wounds that one can inflict on another, and one of the hardest to heal. Amma says that many have lost their faith in spiritual teachers and spirituality because of these incidents. But she has counseled those so wounded not to lose faith or give up hope—that the energy they dedicated to their spiritual practice, even under a false teacher, was not wasted. She says, "The power you have acquired through your spiritual practices is still there, because, unlike material gain, what you have gained through your own efforts cannot be lost.

"Only being in the presence of a Self-realized master can heal the deep wounds of the heart, which have been caused by a false guru or spiritual teacher. A competent healer is someone whose inner eye is opened—one who is able to penetrate deep within a person's mind to clearly see the problems, in order to remove them."

By saying this, Amma does not mean that the rest of us need to have a guru or can't go directly to God, or work with ourselves.

Amma says, "We most certainly have to work with ourselves, but the guidance of a realized master is invaluable and should not be underestimated. No subject can be mastered without a teacher except by a very small number of exceptionally bright students. This principle is true in spirituality also, but even more so because of the extreme subtlety of the subject, God or Self.

"Unlike other subjects that can be learned intellectually, true spirituality must be transmitted from a master to a disciple. This is because the essence of it is the experience of oneness with something entirely transcendental. The intellect has an important role to play, but it can go only so far. It has its limitations. The master will show the way, but it is entirely the responsibility of the student to do the walking. When the student has gone as far as he or she can through their own effort, the master's grace will reveal the truth."

"A person so healed as a result of spiritual betrayal," Amma says, "will receive the necessary strength to prevent them from ever

MA Center Darshan Hall, San Ramon, California

When Amma visits her main ashram in the United States, the atmosphere is that of a sacred and joyous festival. While Amma hugs continuous streams of people twice a day, her monastics sing sacred devotional songs called bhajans.

being hurt again, because they will no longer be vulnerable to those psychological wounds. Sincere seekers who have the mental strength, courage, and spiritual understanding to overcome their initial shock and disappointment, realize that they made an unfortunate mistake in trusting a false teacher. The genuine seeker will immediately leave the false teacher and search for a perfect master, who can lead him or her to the goal of God-realization.

"Such a seeker will certainly find a real master. The master will appear in his or her life, without them having to wander about looking for a teacher. This will happen because of the disciple's sincerity and intense longing."

Many people have called Amma a saint or sage and believe that she is a great master, a reincarnation of Divine Mother, Krishna, Christ, Buddha, or Ramakrishna Paramahansa Ramakrishna. When asked if she believes this about herself, she responded that she basically did not want to claim anything or that she was any particular incarnation of a god or goddess.

Amma said, "A person who studies law becomes a lawyer; a person who studies medicine becomes a doctor. So a person who knows the Self is ordinarily known as a saint or a sage. So it depends on each person's experience. Some people see Mother as Krishna; some others see Mother as Christ or Buddha or Divine Mother. Because God's nature is infinite, God can also have infinite forms and so may not assume the same form each time. In the past God appeared on this earth in the form of Krishna or Rama or Christ or Buddha.

"Mother is just an offering to the world and wants to be available to everyone. That's more important. Just to give and give and give. Mother is like a pure lake. Whoever wants to come to take a bath can take a bath. Or if somebody wants to drink water from it,

Amma leaving San Ramon hall after hugging thousands

quench their thirst, they can do that. Or if someone wants to spit, they can do that as well!

"There are different kinds of people. Some people are like crystal and some others are like clay, some are like coal, and some others are like mud. So when you try to refine them, remold them, some can be really refined, integrated, and uplifted. They will become an image of the master and will become an offering.

"But some will crumble into pieces in that process of remolding and may get destroyed—like mud, which becomes hardened when it is exposed to sunlight."

It is an understatement to say that Amma over the past twenty years has experienced the extreme of human mental conditions. Some people have come to her with the mental clarity and dedication to realize their divinity. Others have come to her who are deeply disturbed mentally or who are completely insane. As her early life reveals, many such disturbed people have criticized and abused her.

But Amma says, "People define Mother in different ways, but Mother has nothing to do with that. They are throwing their own mud, their own dust. It is their own mental stuff. It doesn't matter who says what. If Mother listens to what others say then she will not be able to do her work. Mother's sole mission is to love and serve.

"Some people know when they see the rain clouds and stay there. They want to be drenched in that. They want to feel the raindrops, the coolness. People may say that the greatest sacrifice of Christ was to be on the cross. And some people say that He did a lot of miracles and took on the sin of common people. But the greatest sacrifice Christ performed was to live in the midst of ordinary people with bestial tendencies. And living with them, finally transforming them into God. That is the biggest sacrifice that Christ did.

"Mother is like that. In the process of making pots, many pots will break. We cannot blame the potter for that but the clay. So it depends on each one's understanding, attitude, and maturity. People will throw all their dirt and mud on the master saying, 'It is not me, it is the potter.' "

Whom *can* you trust? What are the qualities of an authentic spiritual master? Many seek the answers to these important questions, because in an age steeped in materialism and increased spiritual cynicism, we are starving spiritually. The Dalai Lama once advised Westerners to study a person's life for at least ten years to determine his or her spiritual credibility as an enlightened teacher.

Amma gives the following advice to people trying to discern the qualities of an authentic spiritual leader: "A true spiritual master is beyond the mind and the ego. In such a master, all sexual energy has been converted into pure vital energy, which he or she uses for the ultimate good of the world. A master is someone who has moved out of the sex center, which is the lowest center of existence, to the highest center of existence—to the crown chakra located in the brain.

"All desires exist in the mind. Once the mind is dissolved, there can be no question of having any desires. In that state no trace of desire remains. The so-called gurus or spiritual teachers who exploit their disciples, sexually or otherwise, or who try to force their ideas on people, are not true masters—far from it. They are still strongly identified with their minds and their desires."

Swami Paramatmananda says, "Amma recommends celibacy to those who feel they can practice it. She says that one should follow it according to one's own capacity. She feels that the energy that each of us has can be used in any way, but if we want to raise our consciousness to a higher than normal level, much of our energy has to be channeled into doing that. Sex is the greatest consumer of our energy. If we can succeed in sublimating it to a more refined, subtle purpose, our progress will be quicker. That is, however, not for everyone. Each one has to decide for him or herself.

"Mother's experience is that when sexual energy is redirected and bears fruit in Self-knowledge, the sexual urge ceases to exist in the glory and intense blissfulness of union with God."

Before meeting Amma in 1992, Beverley Noia was an adjunct professor of religious studies at Regis University, a Jesuit institution in Denver, Colorado. She specialized in Eastern religions and lectured about the spiritual paths in Hinduism and Buddhism.

Beverley told her students about the value of having a realized Being as a spiritual teacher. "But," she said, "I would emphasize how hard it is to find such a person, and how risky it is to entrust your soul's direction to someone less than that—especially someone who claims to be realized, but isn't. People haven't the experience that might help them see through the shams. Their hunger for spiritual growth makes them eager seekers, and thus easy prey."

When she first heard about Amma in 1992, she was suspicious that Amma was just another con artist who wanted to attract gullible people. "I watched Amma for a long time the day I first met her, waiting to see some sign of falseness, something that would tip me off. Instead, time after time, I saw the opposite: I saw concern and compassion in her long gazes at those in pain. And I saw her do this for hours and hours without a break. Someone nearby me murmured, 'And to think, this is what she does, day in and day out, all over the world—and it's been going on for years and years!' It was staggering."

When Beverley became fully convinced that Amma was genuine she sold her house, gave up her job, and moved to the Amri-tapuri Ashram in India. Amma gave her the spiritual name Janani. Presently Beverley travels all over the world with her as one of the official photographers of her world tours.

Janani's healthy skepticism held her in good stead. However, in the early 1980s a young and gentle woman named Victoria experienced a devastating betrayal by a renowned spiritual teacher.

Korean by birth, Victoria moved to the United States when she was a teenager. Raised a devout Roman Catholic, she went to Mass every day for sixteen years, and greatly admired the ideal Christian life that Koreans lived. But she became disappointed with the Catholics she met in America and left the church in search of a deeper spirituality. She went to study with a famous monastic spiritual teacher who had taken vows of celibacy.

She said she benefited from doing the meditative spiritual practices he taught, but that she also began hearing rumors about the man's sexual exploitations. She finally left the organization, feeling sadness and disappointment.

She said, "At first, I didn't believe what people were saying. Although I heard the rumors for years, I didn't believe them. I thought, 'How could a great being like that behave in a way that would destroy his mission?' It didn't make any sense to me. After my teacher passed away in 1982, I had a realization of the truth from within. I was completely devastated and felt a terrible betrayal."

As a result, Victoria rejected everything he had taught her and stopped chanting and meditating. She and her disillusioned friends decided that they would visit all the different spiritual teachers—as a form of entertainment. "That was my form of rebellion against God," she said.

In 1987, a friend informed her that a supposed saint, an Indian lady (Amma), was coming to San Francisco for the first time. Victoria decided to see this Indian lady in order to be "entertained." On the morning she met Amma, she waited in the back of a small room with about twenty other people. She expected to be there only a few minutes and had to be at work a half hour later.

Victoria said she was not prepared for the impact of Amma's presence. "Mother looked around the room, and as soon as she saw me, the universe immediately stopped. I saw infinity in her eyes and went into a deep state of meditation for two hours.

"Being in her presence was an intoxicating feeling of bliss. I tried to get up to leave to go to work, but Mother called me to her lap. It wasn't easy, because all the past sorrows of betrayal came up. But intuitively, I realized that if anyone could heal this wound, it would be her.

"The first thing she said to me was, 'If you want to ask me a question, I will see you in private.' She touched the most sensitive, deepest part of me. I just burst into tears and was in her lap for quite a while, sobbing my heart out, letting out all the sorrow and pain. Mother's sari became completely drenched with my tears. Interestingly enough, I didn't have to ask any question—there was no need. She had healed my deepest wounds."

Ramana Erickson, his sister, and his mother had lived trustingly in a spiritual leader's community from the time he was nine years old until he was twenty-one. When scandals involving his spiritual teacher became known, Ramana experienced a real bitterness and anger toward all spiritual teachers. He thought they were all fakes and phonies who only wanted to have sex and take people's money. He turned his back on spirituality and moved to New York City to become an actor.

His mother, Swami Shraddhananda Saraswati, was very involved in becoming a swami and was unaware of the teacher's inappropriate behavior. When she finally learned of the many scandals, she was greatly shocked and disillusioned. In 1988, her friends told her about Amma. They said she was a great saint. Out of curiosity Swami went to see her, but not with the intention of seeking another spiritual teacher.

Amma told Swami Shraddhananda that once a person becomes disillusioned or loses faith, it is very difficult to get it back again. Swami said, "When she told me that, I was so discouraged. I thought, 'You are a saint. Certainly you have the power to erase this agony.' I was particularly worried about my children. But to make a long story short, she did erase the agony. The disillusionment evaporated in Amma's presence."

Swami Shraddhananda learned from Amma the importance of having humility and compassion. She said, "My former teacher was more dramatic and fiery. I thought he had compassion, but he didn't exhibit humility. It is so important to have a humble and very pure teacher.

"Most significantly, Amma practices what she preaches. I thought my other teacher did, but he didn't. It was terrible news to find out that he wasn't practicing what he preached."

Amma says that a true master, even though he or she is beyond all laws and limitations, must strictly adhere to moral and ethical codes. Only then will the teacher be a good example. Amma said, "If the spiritual teacher says, 'I can do whatever I like. Simply obey me and do as I tell you,' this will only harm the disciple. All the great masters of the past—the ancient saints and sages— were living examples of our highest and most noble values. The disciples need a living example, an embodiment of the divine qualities, to look up to. A true master, therefore, places great importance on morality and ethics."

It took a great deal of effort for Swami Shraddhananda to persuade her son, Ramana, to meet Amma for the first time. Ramana said that when his mother first showed him a picture of Amma, he just laughed. "My mom kept insisting, 'You have to meet her, you have to meet her, you have to meet her.' I kept saying no! I was disillusioned and getting fed up with the whole world."

After much pleading from his mother, he finally consented to see Amma. On his twenty-sixth birthday, he went with his sister to join his mother in a retreat Amma was holding in Eureka, California. When he walked into the retreat room, he saw many faces of people he knew who had studied with his former teacher, and all his negative feelings arose. He wanted to leave, but his mother grabbed him and made him stay.

"She is a strong-willed person," he said. "For a little while I watched Amma from the back of the room, but she did absolutely nothing for me. My mom insisted that I go up to get a hug. I really fought with her on this. But I said, 'Okay, if you'll stop nagging me.' "

As he got in the darshan line he decided that there was no way he would bow to her in the East Indian tradition of acknowledging a saint. He would thank her for making his mother so happy. Then he would shake her hand and leave. "When it was my turn to put my head in Amma's lap, I was feeling embarrassed, bitter, and angry. When she first hugged me I thought, 'I will just wait until she is done.' When she finally let my head up, I said, 'Do you speak Hindi?' And Amma said, 'Hindi?' She laughed and threw my head back down in her lap. When she did, something very strange happened to me. The whole negative monologue that was going on in my head just suddenly stopped. There was just a silence, like a void. I couldn't even think.

"When Amma finally let me up again, she took some sandalwood paste and pressed it between my eyes. When she did, I felt a tremendous transfer of energy, from her into me. I was expecting nothing—I was expecting her to be a total sham. To suddenly feel this power was unbelievable.

"At the time that this power entered me, this understanding came to me that this person was in touch with the Truth, the Truth that I have always been searching for. The next thing I knew, I was asking Mother what sort of spiritual practice I should be doing. I couldn't believe it. It was such a miracle. I had never experienced anything like it. Then I read in her biography that she had licked a leper's wounds. I thought to myself, either she is completely psychotic, or she is the greatest thing ever. I have to go see where she lives."

In November 1988, Ramana went to visit Amma in India.

Ramana said his past spiritual teacher had shady characters in top positions around him. When he first went to India, he was cautious. He did not want to suffer another betrayal. He observed Amma and her swamis very closely for a long time, checking for any signs of corruption. Since that time he has lived a number of years at the Amritapuri Ashram in India.

Stephen Bodian, former editor of *Yoga Journal* magazine, was raised in a traditional Jewish family that had a healthy respect for religion. He became deeply interested in Zen Buddhism and was ordained and practiced as a Zen priest for a number of years. During the ten-year period he was editor of *Yoga Journal* (1984–1994), Stephen interviewed many spiritual teachers, including Amma. After visiting Amma a number of times, he had *Yoga Journal* do a special feature on her.

The first time Stephen visited her, in 1987, he was struck by her totally egoless nature. "I realized she was the pure embodiment of unconditional love, and I felt a tremendous amount of power, joy, and bliss emanate from her. Ten years later, I was in the darshan line more than twenty feet away from her, and even at that distance, I felt my heart chakra being opened by an overwhelming wave of her unconditional love. It put me into a state of ecstasy."

MA CENTER, SAN RAMON, CALIFORNIA

Amma's San Ramon Ashram, founded in 1989, was set up primarily to help organize her world tours and retreats. The small group of people living at the ashram today come from various religious traditions, and they have made a conscious choice to dedicate their life to God and selfless service.

Cindy is one such person. Before having met Amma, she was ignorant of Eastern spirituality. As a child, Cindy was raised as a Unitarian Protestant by an open-minded family who taught her that God is love, and to acknowledge the universal validity of all traditional spiritual paths.

Until she met Amma in June 1996, she had spent many years immersed in New Age spirituality and thought of herself as a "Christian-Buddhist-New Ager." As a New Ager, she believed that the most important barometer of God-attainment in this world was the degree to which joy, love, and pleasure existed in her life. Cindy thought the degree to which her dreams and desires were fulfilled was a measure of her spiritual success or failure, but she has since learned that the Hindu tradition teaches that it is our continuous materialistic desires that keep us from realizing our true Self.

"I learned that in order to awaken to my Divine Self, the following qualities had to be put into practice: selflessness, self-sacrifice, love, devotion, patience, tolerance, faith, surrender, humility, and acceptance."

Like many New Agers, Cindy questioned whether the sufferings of great masters like Amma, Jesus Christ, and Buddha were necessary. She and others at the ashram have learned from Amma's life and teachings that when a master is in a physical body, he or she follows the laws of nature.

Amma told her spiritual seekers, "Children, once realization is attained, some beings merge with eternity. Very few of them come down. Who would like to come down after having entered the Ocean of Bliss? In order to come down from that state from which there is no return, it is necessary to have something to hold on to, a determined thought (mental resolve or sankalpa). Only a few who can make that sankalpa to descend will come down.

"That mental resolve is compassion, love, or selfless service to suffering humanity. If you do not want to listen and respond to the call of those sincere seekers and the cry of those who are suffering in the world, and if you want to remain in the impersonal state and do not want to be compassionate, it is all right. You can remain there.

"Once you've come down from oneness with God, you play the role well. You live and work hard for the uplift of all humanity. You'll have problems, obstacles, difficult situations. You'll also have to face abuses, scandals, calumny, but you do not care because although externally you look like everybody else, internally you are different, totally different. Inside you are one with the Supreme Truth. Therefore, you're untouched, unaffected. Having become one with the very source of energy itself, you work tirelessly, healing and soothing the deep wounds of those who come to you.

"You give peace and happiness to everyone. Your way of living life, your renunciation, love, compassion, and selflessness give inspiration to others to want to experience what you experience. In order to express compassion and love and perform selfless service to inspire others to experience those divine qualities, one must have a body. Once a body is taken, it has to take its natural course.

"The mahatma's body is different from an ordinary person's. If he so wills, he can keep the body as long as he wishes without being afflicted by disease and suffering. But he consciously makes the body undergo all experiences that an ordinary human being undergoes. Therein lies his greatness! A God-realized soul gives the body to the world, and it goes its natural course. But it can be made to do exceptional things.

"Didn't Krishna get hurt during the Mahabharata war? Didn't He fight eighteen times with Jarasandha, the powerful and cruel king? Finally, He diplomatically left the battlefield. He could have killed Jarasandha if He wanted to, but Krishna didn't. Remember, it was an arrow shot by an ordinary hunter which put an end to Krishna's life in this world.

"Jesus was executed on the cross. Both of them could have prevented the events which put an end to their bodies, but they let everything happen in the natural course of events. They were willing to surrender. However, this does not mean that the natural course is inevitable or unavoidable for them, as it is for ordinary humans. If they had wished, they could have avoided all bitter experiences. Being all-powerful, they could have effortlessly destroyed those who opposed them, but they wanted to set an example. They wanted to show the world that it is possible to live with the highest values of life even while undergoing all the problems that an ordinary human has."

In the United States, many people believe that if they just had a million dollars, all their problems would be solved. But other people, when they discover that worldly possessions do not bring them the joy they had expected, sell off their hard-earned possessions to pursue true happiness. Darsana is such a person.

Darsana is African-American. She was born to poor parents in a small town in rural Oklahoma. Her father was a Baptist, and her mother a Methodist. When Darsana was ten, she wanted to convert to Catholicism. Eventually she got an M.B.A degree from the University of Detroit, a Jesuit institution.

When she was thirteen, her family moved to Michigan. At that time, she became very interested in overcoming the poverty in which she was living. She felt the only way out for her was to go to school. She said, "My mother always said, 'You must educate yourself in order to provide for yourself.' "

When she was twenty-two, she got a job at General Motors. Being highly intelligent, she worked her way up to director of operations and reporting for the Employee Benefit Plans Administration Section. She now had a salary, a bonus, a company car, a husband, and a son.

"But I came to realize that when I finally lived in the right neighborhood, in a five-bedroom house with five baths, three fireplaces, and a swimming pool—that it was the most lonely, unhappy time in my life.

"I thought all of those things would give me happiness, but none of them did. To realize that was painful because then I didn't know where to go or what to do. One night I got home from work, and a voice inside me said, 'But don't you know that one day you are going to die?' And then—I really didn't know what to do."

Darsana ended up quitting her job and selling her house. Then one day a friend of her sister's introduced her to a swami who started teaching her aspects of Eastern spirituality. This was a real turning point in her life.

She bought a ticket to India via Africa, since her ancestry was African.

Darsana felt India was her spiritual home, and she lived in an ashram there for some time before coming back to the United States. She had given up the hope of finding a living master. But in June 1994, she met Amma.

Darsana now lives at the San Ramon Ashram, working on the AIMS Hospital project as part of her selfless service.

Darsana views Amma as a flawless mirror whose mere presence reflects another person's state of consciousness. Darsana says that in Amma's presence, "You see yourself with all of your limitations, all of your weaknesses, everything—against that divine mirror with all of its perfection and fullness. One's limitations are so blatantly clear. And you know from scriptures that those are the limitations you have placed on yourself. Then the work becomes removing the limitations."

Amma is a mirror to people of all faiths.

On July 1, 1998, Sister Rose Mercurio and eight other Catholic women drove from St. Louis, Missouri, to Chicago, Illinois, to receive Amma's blessing. It was Sister Rose's first time meeting Amma.

Coming from a traditional Catholic background, Sister Rose was initially overwhelmed with the smells, Indian customs, and people. She found it impressive that thousands of people would sit so patiently for Amma's darshan.

"I was overcome by Amma's accessibility. She was available to all people. Unlike higher church dignitaries that I have known who are surrounded with ceremony and seem inaccessible."

Sister Rose, as the pastoral minister to Our Lady of Good Counsel Church in St. Louis, visits the sick, gives communion, and teaches preventive health classes. She says, "Amma affirms in me what I believe—that there is a God in each of us, longing to touch the God in everyone else. She has responded to the Divinity, which is in each of us, and she challenges me to aspire to that potential. My background as a Roman Catholic has laid the foundation for this belief. Amma simply urges me forward."

Chapter 14

SPIRITUAL BOOT CAMP
THE 1999 NORTH INDIAN TOUR

On February 20, after a light afternoon rain, the sun broke through dark gray clouds and cast a majestic double rainbow that arched high above the Amritapuri Ashram temple, spanning miles of palm trees. I took it as an auspicious sign. Amma was about to embark upon the grueling, six-week North Indian tour. Her advice to those going was that they should have the attitude that the trip is a spiritual pilgrimage.

There is no substitute for authentic experience. At this juncture, I journeyed as a pilgrim as well as a chronicler of Amma's life. Traveling with Amma in close association, and subjectively experiencing, in some small degree, the rigors she goes through year after year, I was helped to better understand her life more fully. However, becoming a pilgrim opened me to the possibility of personal transformation as well.

There was a major shift in energy at the ashram as I and 350 other people readied ourselves to go with Amma on the tour. The following day, we caravanned in six huge, Indian-style excursion

Map of India

Amma's 1999 North India tour started at Amritapuri Ashram in Kerala. Amma's caravan traveled north to Hyderabad, Pune, Mumbai, all the way to New Delhi, then East to Calcutta.

buses, two jeeps, and Amma's car, to ten cities, as far north as New Delhi and then to Calcutta, our last destination. By the end of this journey, Amma would have hugged close to a quarter of a million people, given private audiences to numerous political leaders, and visited many devotees' homes to bless their meditation rooms.

We were a traveling United Nations, consisting of 150 Indians; swamis, swaminis, brahmacharis, and other long-term ashram residents; and 220 other people, mostly from America and Europe, with another 10 percent coming from countries such as Korea, Japan, South Africa, Canada, Malaysia, Chile, Argentina, Armenia, Mexico, Iran, Israel, Brazil, and Turkey.

In preparation for the trip, Amma's huge ashram kitchen was disassembled. Hardworking men packed up huge metal cooking pots the size of hot tubs, portable gas burners and fuel, multiple fifty-pound bags of rice, tea for chai, water, miscellaneous food staples, and cooking implements, which they loaded on top of a couple of the buses. Spiritual books and other items to be sold at Amma's various programs were placed under the bus seats. Next, 350 bedrolls and a small piece of luggage for each pilgrim were secured on top of the other buses.

For the previous five years Jani, an Israeli woman, and Priyan, a Lebanese man, had organized many of the details for Amma's North Indian tour. It was said jokingly that Amma put them together to help create world peace because they come from two countries that normally don't get along. Their Herculean task was to make sure that everyone had their general needs taken care of, and that each person was assigned a place on the buses and had floor space to sleep on at the different sites along the way.

People drawn to go on this pilgrimage were: Indians who came from Hindu, Muslim, and Christian traditions and who had found in Amma the living truth of the Vedas, the Koran, and

Jesus' life and teachings; and Westerners from Jewish and Christian traditions who had previously had an interest in Hindu or Buddhist spirituality.

Out of respect, because we were traveling with Amma, we were asked to wear white clothing—the traditional color of purity.

The trip was going to be rough for those of us who were not used to living an ascetic life. We were told we would have to give up all of our concepts of comfort, privacy, and of being able to hide our faults from other people, because there would be no place to hide. All negative tendencies of the rational mind and ego would tend to come to the surface, like anger and impatience over not getting our needs met.

If taken in the right spirit, the journey would be transformative—purifying our minds and cleansing us of bad karma. The pilgrimage would provide us with many spiritual lessons in nonattachment, patience, self-control, and equanimity. As spiritual pilgrims, we would be challenged to remain compassionate and loving when interacting with all kinds of people, in all sorts of situations.

We were advised about potential health hazards regarding food and water. It was also highly recommended that we take along mosquito nets, bug repellant, and either allopathic or homeopathic remedies for malaria. The medication would be needed when we would stay in Mumbai (Bombay) and other northern cities known to have outbreaks of malaria.

Two months before I left for India, numerous New Age catalogs advertising new millennium spiritual excursions to the Caribbean arrived in my mailbox. These trips were advertised as an opportunity for a person to do deep inner exploration. This "inner exploration" included five-star accommodations where the mind could listen to famous authors speak on spiritual subjects while the body got to lie in the sun and get pampered.

My body/mind was terrified at the thought of suffering the hardships of going to India and fiercely battled with my soul to go on one of those Caribbean cruises. The soul having won, it ordered the body/mind to pack a pollution mask for Delhi, a Therm-a-Rest inflatable mattress and pillow for sleeping on floors, rehydration salts for tropic heat, megavitamins, and other high-potency medications in case of sickness.

Priyan and Jani told me that it was only by Amma's grace that such a dangerous trip through India could be undertaken. In previous years, they said, the monastics had to put poisonous thorns on top of the buses when passing through a certain Indian state to prevent bandits, hiding in trees above the road, from stealing the luggage off the top of the buses.

Priyan said that in 1997, as they started out from Ahmadabad on their way to New Delhi, more and more people requested special stops to go to the toilet. It is a long trip and normally takes twenty-four hours of driving. Westerners in particular have to be very careful about the food they eat and the water they drink, because one can easily get diarrhea.

He said soon there was a crisis. "At first we had only two people with diarrhea, then twenty, then forty, then fifty. The road was crowded with vehicles, so there was no privacy alongside the road, and people had to walk a bit to find trees or bushes. I was very worried because we were losing so much time stopping. The next day's program in New Delhi was starting at 6:00 A.M., and we were expected to be in Delhi at 10:00 P.M. that evening. But by 6:00 A.M. the next morning, we still hadn't reached Delhi.

"I ran to a swami in one of the cars and told him that I was not able to get the buses to move because we would stop for half an hour and then drive for five minutes. 'Please, tell me what I should do?' Swami just shrugged and said, 'Later, later.' So I jumped in the bus, and ten minutes later we stopped again. This time I came out of the bus very quickly and rushed passed his car. He called out to me, but I said, 'Swamiji, just one minute, my time has come!' "

Priyan said one Indian brahmachari who looks for the humor in every situation ran around interviewing everyone as if he were a reporter for a television show. The brahmachari said, "So, how many times did you go tonight? You DID?" The Indian made everyone laugh, and after some time, everybody saw the humor of it.

Fortunately, a message had been sent ahead to the New Delhi devotees, who were waiting for the caravan with antibiotics. Within a day or two, people were back to normal.

After hearing that story, I put out a strong intention to God that I find the humor in the challenging situations that may lay ahead on the 1999 tour, as I would be a spiritual pilgrim as well as a biographer.

Because of a bad back, I opted to pay a little extra money to ride with two other American women in one of the ashram jeeps instead of in a bus with all Western women. However, the jeep had no seat belts, and so many times, my body bounced up and down like a rubber ball as we drove thousands of miles over countless potholes. Miraculously, my spine stayed intact the whole trip. Indian swamis and brahmacharis were assigned to ride in our jeep, which provided me with a unique opportunity to better understand Indian culture and the depth of the dedication the swamis have for the rigors of spiritual life.

On the first day we traveled over twenty hours, stopping every three or four hours to take breaks. Our first destination was Mysore. By late afternoon, we started up a mountain pass that would take

us out of South India. Alongside the narrow road, clusters of
adorable-looking monkeys held their babies and eyed us inquisi-
tively as we passed by. At the end of the tour, I would have a unique
encounter with a monkey near the Kali temple in Dakshineswar.

The tests that come up for a sincere seeker on a spiritual pilgrimage like the North Indian tour are meant to help the individual
discover his or her true Self, or soul. Such tests help to weaken
the ego so that the real Self can manifest.

The spiritual tests began the very first day, when we were
given the opportunity to learn how to be unaffected by outer
circumstances.

At dusk, the Holy Mother had the buses pull off the main road
onto a dirt road so that we could meditate and have a chai tea
break before going on to Mysore. It was at least thirty to forty
degrees cooler on the mountain, and we were only wearing light-
weight tropical clothes. Amma didn't coddle us by saying, 'Darling children, let's go someplace warmer.' Instead, she sat down
on the damp, cold ground and went into a deep meditation. Normally, I would be shivering too much to be able to meditate, but
surprisingly I found that being in her presence, I was able to meditate a short time without being aware of my physical body and its
discomfort.

One bus carrying Western men had broken down earlier in
the afternoon. They did not make it to the meditation, and it
would take them many additional hours to reach Mysore safely.

Harry (not his real name) was on that bus. From the very
beginning, he suffered physical, emotional, and spiritual pain
that he had never known before. He was a middle-aged American
man who weighed two hundred pounds. He was put in a row of
seats with two other men who also weighed close to two hundred
pounds. He said that those same three seats would have been very

Evening meditation with Amma, 1999 North Indian tour
We sat in meditation on dry, rocky land, bathed in the light of an orange setting sun, rimmed in fluorescent blue. Amma says meditation is the technique that allows you to shut the doors and windows of the senses so that you can look within and see your Self.

uncomfortable for two men, let alone three. Another pilgrim who had been on several North Indian tours said that by comparison, an American Greyhound bus would seem like heaven.

Harry came on the pilgrimage to find out who he was.

"It was a huge risk for me," he said. "One way or the other, I had to find out if I was a really good or a really bad person. When we first started, nobody knew each other. But as we got to know one another, we slowly but surely found this incredible tolerance and love for each other that only seems to come through this kind of intense experience, where you are thrown into an excruciating situation, where you don't get a lot of sleep, and where things in which you are used to finding comfort are taken away from you. You have to dig deep into your heart and soul to find the strength to permanently change."

Sri Pati, a young American man from Philadelphia, was on the same bus with Harry. He said, "We learned empathy when some of the men got violently ill and really needed to rest. They would lie down in the center aisle of the bus, and all the other men would pitch in and contribute blankets or pillows and then softly step around or over them to get past while they recovered."

Because Harry's bus had broken down, one of the other five buses was sent to pick them up. But before it could be sent, everyone on that bus had to get off and remove all their luggage. Those people were reassigned to one of the four remaining buses, which now had to accommodate twelve extra people. As there were no seats available, they had to stand in the aisles for the rest of the eight-hour journey.

One day, while we were eating lunch at one of the program sites, an Indian brahmachari asked me why I was on the North Indian tour. I told him that I was writing Amma's biography.

With a shocked look on his face, he hastily asked, "Who are

you?" Actually, his question was one that any sincere spiritual seeker needs to ask him or herself.

Who am I? I pondered how to answer him. If I told him my birth name and listed my writing and academic credentials, it would be a superficial, egotistical answer. If he was looking for signs of spiritual attainment as criteria for writing Amma's biography, I did not have even a pundit's degree in religious studies, nor did I wear the traditional orange garb of a swami. Frankly, my body had been perpetually sick in India, and I looked like a sadhu who had rubbed gray ash all over his body. However, in my case, there was no "holy glow" accompanying the ashen color.

So I avoided answering the brahmachari.

But later, the correct response to his question popped in my mind: "I Am That!"—the soul, pure consciousness. Yes, of course, the Vendantic answer, "I Am That!"—so simple and yet so truthful. I started laughing (God does have a sense of humor). It is easy enough to say the words "I Am That!" but it is another thing to deeply experience and realize the truth of the Self.

Shortly after this incident, I was riding in the jeep with an Indian swami and a brahmachari whom I had not met before. Partway into the journey, the brahmachari asked what country I came from, and why I had come on the trip. I told him I had come because I was writing Amma's biography.

He thought for a moment, and with a deeply puzzled look on his face, he said, "You know, it is very unusual that Mother would allow someone to write about her who was not close to her."

Repressing the urge to giggle, I smilingly replied, "Do you mean physically close, or spiritually close? You sound like another brahmachari who asked me, 'Who are *you?*'" By this time I could not help but chuckle outloud. He also began to laugh, and apologized for his inference.

Great sages of India, including Amma, teach that they are not the body, and that their consciousness spans the whole universe. They are omnipresent—having merged their conscious-ness with the premordial sound of Om (Aum). Thus, anyone can be spiritually close to a great master merely by concentrated thought on them, as they are within us, and all around us, as pure Consciousness.

However, the various Indian responses made it clear that they perceived my being Amma's biographer to be radically unortho-dox. In the subjective mode of spiritual seeker, it felt more and more like I was living a contemporary reenactment of biblical times.

Elaine Pagels, author of *The Gnostic Gospels*, relates that in the Gospel of Thomas, St. Peter complained to Jesus Christ that Mary Magdalene should not associate with Jesus or the other male disciples because she was not a man, and thus not their spir-itual equal.

Dr. Pagels said the Christian Gnostics taught essentially the same truths concerning enlightenment and spiritual equality as have been expounded by the great Indian sages. But as the Church became a political power, two or three hundred years after Christ died, the Gnostic teachings were condemned as heresy, and women became spiritually suppressed.

It became apparent to me that deeply ingrained spiritual preju-dice exists in India as well as in the West. But my experience taught me that Amma creates situations so as to help uproot such tendencies—by bringing men and women from all over the world to work together. Through infinite patience, and by example, Amma in her role as a sage demonstrates spiritual equality. Never once did I experience her treating anyone as inferior, or incapable of enlightenment.

Thus, I began to understand the importance of learning directly from a sage. It became easy to see why spiritual inequality grips our present consciousness. When a great master leaves the body, disciples are left in charge, and few of them have a vision equal to that of the sage. Like what happened in Christianity over thousands of years, many in spiritual authority were still striving to be saints. Consequently such authorities, still ruled by the ego and fragmented rational consciousness, based their knowledge on an intellectual interpretation of truth, not on a direct experience of the Truth.

My encounters in India made me appreciate deeply the work Amma is doing in our world today to bring back that clear vision. The greatest gift has been for me to study and write about her life while she is still in the body—to observe a great master working with disciples and devotees to help expand their consciousness.

At Amma's Pune Ashram, several different Indian brahmacharis who were on the tour shared what the spiritual challenges were for them. One young man said that before they left the Amritapuri Ashram, all the male monastics met with Swami Amritaswarupananda. Swami told them the test was to see where each one stood on their spiritual path as they mingled with society. He said the real purpose of the tour was to gain energy, not to lose it. Monastics lose energy, he said, if they get caught in worldly thoughts and forget the real purpose of renunciation.

During our stay at Pune, Swami Amritaswarupananda severely injured his back and had to be taken to a hospital in Bombay. He would not be able to travel with Amma for the rest of the trip. Because of his deep love and devotion to her, this was an almost unbearable sacrifice. We were all deeply saddened by the news of his plight.

By the time we reached Bombay, many more people had become ill, and Amma's voice grew more hoarse with each passing day. Thousands of people asked not only for her hug but also for her advice on problems they were having.

Amma was like someone who was plugged into a high-voltage transformer that never shuts down. At each city, she did two programs a day. After finishing her night programs, which lasted until three or four in the morning, she would travel to a number of devotees' homes so as to bless their prayer rooms. By this time it would be six or seven in the morning. She then would give many private interviews to the various political dignitaries. At eleven, she would begin all over again to hug people at the morning program. It hardly seemed possible that she could sleep more than an hour or two, so packed was her schedule.

No matter how much physical pain Amma might be suffering, or how grueling her schedule, she lovingly nurtured us by taking us to two rivers to swim, and fed us *prasad* a number of times from her very own hands. Those precious moments with her sweetened the bitterness of the journey. Observing her capacity for selfless sacrifice left an indelible impression on my mind. Certainly if Amma could sacrifice so much for so many people, the least I could do was to never feel sorry for myself for any discomfort I might experience on the journey.

Accommodations (for sleeping on the floor) on the North Indian tour varied from damp, freshly curing cement floors, in one of Amma's new primary schools, to dusty linoleum-tiled floors, to one gigantic marble floor in a marriage palace in Bangalore. It gave me a brief experience of what living the life a wandering Indian sadhu might be like. Wandering sadhus are holy persons who never stay long enough in one place to ever become attached to it. It taught me that our real home is not a place but a state of mind.

At the marriage palace in Bangalore, I slept with 150 women on the marble floor. The rest of the women stayed in ten other small rooms bordering the large hall. These rooms accommodated four or five people each, and also had the only bathrooms,

Amma with starving child, 1999 North Indian tour
On the way back from a river where we stopped to swim, Amma found this poor child and its mother, who had no home or food. Amma had the monastics make arrangements to get food and shelter for them.

which had to service two hundred or more women. Those choosing the smaller rooms had to forego attachment to sleep as well as privacy, because they were asked to keep the door open at all times so that the rest of us could have access to the bathrooms.

By contrast, on our way to New Delhi, we stayed at an orthodox Hindu monastery in Baroda. Our jeep arrived in the middle of the night, much later than the buses. All the women were put in a separate wing of the monastery, overlooking a cow pen. The only sleeping space left was on the porch floor. It was my first experience of being in such close sleeping proximity to holy cows. Because it was dark when I arrived, I could only hear and smell them. All night long, they burped and made the most unusual sounds, like *bah, boo, bbblatt,* as if they were speaking in some kind of Hindi cow language. Not once during the night did I hear a "moo."

At sunrise, the air was filled with the sounds of Hindu monks chanting. In my effort to maintain a prayerful attitude, I very quietly remarked to one young woman that I had never heard such strange sounds coming from cows before. At that precise moment, one cow let out a huge *mooo,* as if trying to prove to me that it *could* speak "normal" cow language.

ROADS INDICATE THE CULTURE OF A NATION

This sign, written in English, was mounted alongside the highway to Hyderabad. I really couldn't say for sure that roads are a clear indicator of a nation's culture. But there are no posted speed limits and almost no police control for the countless reckless drivers that use the Indian roads. By traveling the Indian highways as a pilgrim I learned a number of lessons: to not react emotionally to negative outer circumstances, and to let go the fear of death by always keeping my mind calm and focused on God.

Our jeep driver was exceptional. Even after driving twenty hours a day, on the worst roads, with no one to relieve him, he remained intensely alert and kept a cheerful attitude. On the way to Hyderabad, I finally learned to remain calm and trust his skills. Eventually, I was able to meditate even with an onslaught of aggressive truck drivers that continuously veered onto the wrong side of the road, barely missing our jeep.

The road to Hyderabad was not straight but wound like the folds of a brain. The highway didn't appear to have been constructed to reach "a destination" in the most minimal amount of "time." On the contrary, when we came to an intersection that branched out into three different directions, there were no markers to indicate which of the roads would take us to Hyderabad. Instead, the swami would get out of the jeep and ask the local villagers to point the way.

It was our last day on the road before reaching New Delhi. Early that evening, our jeep and Amma's car stopped next to a dusty field to wait for the buses to arrive. We would meditate and have tea together before continuing to Delhi. It was a most rare moment to be with Amma while waiting for the buses. There were only fifteen of us, and it gave me an opportunity to ask her a few more questions.

For a number of years, I have been fascinated by the Sri Yantra symbol, which at the deepest level represents enlightenment, or Self-realization of one's divinity. In the West, progressive scientists, musicians, and artists have been interested in this symbol, and it was the central symbol I used throughout my book *Mandala: Luminous Symbols for Healing*.

By studying Amma's life—her self-sacrificing love and compassion for all people, her miracles and numerous charities—I felt intuitively that she may be a genuine embodiment of the Sri Yantra symbol: an enlightened being.

The dusty field glowed a twilight orange as fifteen of us sat on the ground around Amma. I explained to her that I was trying to understand the link between her and the Sri Yantra symbol. "Amma, the Bombay scientists feel it is a most important symbol because it contains very advanced mathematical theorems. And the Sri Yantra is an integral part in the installation of your new temples. What is your teaching on the Sri Yantra? Many believe that it represents Aum, the light and sound of consciousness, the Divine Mother as Shakti energy."

Amma replied, "Historically, those who made a ritual Sri

Amma during Devi Bhava, circa 1996
*The Sri Yantra or Sri Chakra behind Amma represents Devi, the
Cosmic Mother. Many in India associate this symbol with Amma
because it is the most appropriate symbol to represent her enlightenment and manifestation as a Divine Mother.*

Yantra out of metal also observed strict vows, like fasting and
celibacy, and wore completely wet clothes during the process.
They chanted special mantras, and as a result of these practices, a
special power was transferred to that yantra. Nowadays, most people use a machine to make the Sri Yantra. Therefore, it is not
imbued with the power of one made in accordance with the
ancient tradition."

However, her answer about the history of the ritual worship or

the making of a metal Sri Yantra symbol was not what I was interested in. How could I explain to her that I had been intuitively
led to believe that *she* was the full embodiment of what the Sri
Yantra symbol represented?

As twilight waned, it took all my courage to boldly pose this
intuition as a direct question. "Amma, you *are* the Sri Yantra, is
this not true?"

She bowed her head and very quietly said, "Yes, yes, yes."

The buses arrived. After tea and meditation, we traveled another
eight hours before reaching New Delhi. Due to road construction,
five of those eight hours were spent in gridlock and stopped traffic.
Never before had I experienced such extreme pollution. If hell had
a road, this was it. Trucks spewed gray-black petrol fumes and the
yellow-green "air" stung my lungs and nose. I wished that I had progressed spiritually enough to consciously stop my breath and go
into deep samadhi.

The assault of this pollution left many of us, including the
Indian monastics, quite sick by the time we arrived in New
Delhi. Amma too was quite sensitive to the dust and extreme pollution. I must confess that after one night in our new accommodations (we were in New Delhi five days in all) I took my charge
card and went to a hotel for three nights to sleep off a fever and
severe bronchial infection.

On the other hand, Amma, in spite of being ill herself, never
once canceled a program.

After I had returned to the group accommodations on the
fourth day, Jani saw that I was having a difficult time. In her
Israeli accent she said, "Judit, if you don't suffar you won't write
a good't book." She was right. You cannot authentically portray
someone else's life without having a genuine experience of it. It
was only by going on the North Indian tour that I began to com-

prehend the magnitude of the sacrifices Amma and her monastics make to relieve the sufferings of humanity.

Many people have asked Amma about the immensity of the trials and tribulations that she has had to confront. They wonder how their own Self-realization could ever take place if they have to undergo so much suffering, which they doubt they could ever be capable of. Amma says, "My own life only shows that it is possible to realize God even under the worst possible circumstances."

The last part of the tour was by train to Calcutta. By the time we departed, there were only two hundred people left. The other pilgrims had departed earlier from Bombay or New Delhi. I was extremely tempted to bail out in Delhi and return home. However, my soul gave me the strength to go on and dragged my limp body with it.

CALCUTTA, THE CITY OF SAINTS

Whistles blowing, the express train to Calcutta rocked, rolled, and clickity-clacked for sixteen hours straight. Amma did not sleep on the train but insisted on giving all two hundred of us darshan—fifteen at a time—in her private car. I asked her how Swami Amritaswarupananda was doing in the hospital, and if he was able to sing yet. She started crying. Her tears were of compassion for her dear disciple's emotional and physical pain. This incident taught me that great souls, like Amma, are deeply sensitive. In their state of expanded awareness, they feel intensely each soul's agony.

So many saints I had only read about and admired had lived in Calcutta; like Mother Teresa, Paramahansa Yogananda, Lahiri

Mahasaya, and Ramakrishna Paramahansa. On our last day in Calcutta, an ashram bus took a few of us to the famous Kali temple in Dakshineswar, where Ramakrishna had his mystical experience of Divine Mother Kali. It was to this same temple that Ramakrishna's disciple Master Mahasaya took Paramahansa Yogananda, and prayed for Yogananda to have an inner vision of the Divine Mother.

I had a strong urge to visit that temple because of my devotion to God as Divine Mother. On the way to the main temple complex, I noticed a group of cute-looking monkeys playing near a miniature temple building that edged the Ganges river. I purchased a small basket, beautifully constructed out of leaves and willow branches, that was filled with bright red hibiscus flowers. Standing behind a low gate in front of the statue of Kali, I presented the basket to the temple priest as an offering to the goddess. He took it, blessed the offering, and returned the basket, filled with *prasad* in the form of thick, cream-colored wafers.

On my way back to the bus, beggars stopped and asked for *prasad*. I gave some of it to a few starving souls and saved a little for friends back in the United States. As I was going toward the path with the monkeys, one large male monkey caught my eye. He aggressively lunged toward me and fought to take the basket of *prasad* from my clutching hands.

He had very bad manners, so I was determined not to give him the few remaining pieces of *prasad*. In that moment, I felt as fearless as the Goddess Kali, and I forcibly held on to the basket. When he would not let go, I went into monkey consciousness. I stood my ground by baring my teeth and hissing at him. He stepped away a bit, then likewise, he bared his teeth and hissed back.

At that moment, a small wave of fear passed over me. Instantly, I decided to let the basket go if he came toward me again. But he didn't. Indians who witnessed the event stood by with gaping mouths. I walked away with the spoils—a broken basket and crushed *prasad*.

After the fact, I learned that monkeys can be quite dangerous, and that they do bite. You are not supposed to look a monkey directly in the eyes, as it will take it as an act of aggression.

In the evening, I went to Amma's final program and received her darshan for the last time in India before returning to the United States. As challenging as the journey had been, I could barely hold back the tears when I thought about leaving. As a spiritual pilgrim, I felt transformed and richly blessed by the experience of a deep spiritual connection with the Indian people, Amma, and with her pilgrims from all over the world.

However, there was no resting for Amma.

The very next day Amma and her monastics began a journey to her ashram on Mauritius Island, located a thousand miles east of Africa, to give hugs to those seeking her healing balm of unconditional love.

॰ॐ॰

HEALING THE HEART
OF THE WORLD

Haloed in splendor, the Divine Mother stood before me. Her face, tenderly smiling, was beauty itself. "Always have I loved thee! Ever shall I love thee!" The celestial tones still ringing in the air, She disappeared.

— PARAMAHANSA YOGANANDA, AUTOBIOGRAPHY OF A YOGI

January 1, 2000

A cool wind lightly brushed my cheeks as I stood on a bluff overlooking the Pacific Ocean. The clear, sunny air was filled with the sound of waves pounding the shore below. I was ending a five-day silent retreat at the Self-Realization Fellowship Hermitage in Encinitas, California. Almost seventy years ago, this hermitage was given to Paramahansa Yogananda by his close disciples. It is the place where Yogananda wrote his famous *Autobiography of a Yogi*, and where he was visited by many great sages and saints.

Having been raised a Roman Catholic, I developed in my youth a deep devotion to Mary the Mother of God. But later in life it was through Yogananda's teachings that I first learned to love, honor, and understand the feminine aspect of God as the Divine Mother. The hermitage land, imbued as it is with holy vibrations, seemed a perfect place to collect my thoughts on what I had learned from writing Amma's biography.

For eleven years I had perceived Amma simply as a sweet "hugging saint." But as her story unfolded, my limited vision of her greatly expanded. It was awesome to discover that Amma was not just a saint, but one of India's most illustrious sages. She heals on a massive scale—far beyond that of any saint or healer I had ever known or read about. The immensity of Amma's global reach made it quite clear to me that she is playing a key role in healing our hearts and fragmented minds so as to help humanity take the next step in the evolution of consciousness.

Amma says that her only religion is love. Although people may come from different religious faiths and have different cultures and ways of thinking, the language of the heart is always the same—and that language is love. The divisions in the minds of individuals, she says, are the cause of division in families, which in turn will be reflected in societies, nations, and the whole world.

I learned that Amma does not merely talk about the problems afflicting society. She demonstrates through example. With the help of her devotees, she has created practical archetypes that incorporate development of the whole person—body, mind, and spirit. There is not a single facet of life that her thousand arms of compassion has not touched nor transformed—be it family life, education, the sciences, medicine, psychology, religion, or the sacred arts.

The family is the key to a successful society. The first to be transformed by Amma's love were her family, relatives, and villagers. Although Amma was abused, she did not herself become an abuser, nor did she run away from her problems. She proved that no one is hopeless, and that love, forgiveness, and patience have real healing power to transform even the hatred of one's enemies.

If Gandhi were alive today, I can only think that he would be absolutely awed by Amma's practical accomplishments in intellectually, spiritually, and materially benefiting Indian women. In so doing, she provides an ideal for the rest of the world.

Married Indian women who have gone to Amma for advice are encouraged to get an education, so that if their husbands should die or leave them, they will be able to support themselves. Penniless widows receive pensions and free houses from her nonprofit trust. And by bringing back into practice the Vedic concept of true spiritual equality, she has empowered women to once again take their rightful place in the spiritual community.

Once Rabindranath Tagore, the famous Indian poet, told Paramahansa Yogananda, "True education is not pumped and crammed in from outward sources, but aids in bringing to the surface the infinite hoard of wisdom within." Both of these men created alternative schools of education based on their deep experiential understanding that the soul brings all past knowledge into its new incarnation. If they were alive today, they would laud Amma's educational efforts.

Having only a fourth-grade education, Amma proved, by her monumental accomplishments, that real knowledge comes from within. Amma has created schools based on the ancient Vedic tradition wherein children are taught to meditate in order to access this inner knowledge. In addition to reading and writing, each child is given the opportunity to develop their innate creativity, so that they can experience life as a joyful celebration and be well prepared to take on the challenges of the world.

The older students in Amma's advanced computing, management, and engineering schools learn all about human character, and exactly what the mind is. They are taught traditional moral and spiritual values, and learn to give part of their time to selfless service and ecological restoration projects.

I learned that material science, like education, is developmentally influenced by the fragmented minds of individuals who make up the field. Amma, in her dialogues with Western-trained scientists, introduced the importance of taking up India's ancient spiritual science of consciousness and sound to gain more complete knowledge about the universe. Western scientists assume that matter and consciousness are separate, but for Amma, only consciousness exists. Her greatest miracle, which is her hugging millions of people each year, in addition to her miracles of changing water into pudding and curing the leper, are examples that show she has gone beyond the known laws of physics. As a living sage, Amma is a legacy for scientists to ponder and study.

In reestablishing true spirituality, Amma continually reminds her children that they are divine and immortal souls—no matter what religion they follow or what country they come from.

Wearing only a simple white sari, Amma eschews titles and pompous shows of religiosity. Time and again, she has demonstrated through her comportment and numerous charities the true humility of an enlightened master. Like the Tibetan Buddhists, Amma believes that one should have an unselfish desire even for enlightenment—that is, one should desire enlightenment so as to help enlighten others.

It has been a great learning as well as a deep healing experience to write Amma's biography.

Stories about the various Christian mystics have nurtured my soul since I was a child. I was particularly drawn to Teresa of Avila, the founder of the Carmelite order, who was a great mystic. When I was a young woman, I dedicated my life to knowing and experiencing God and studied to become a Carmelite nun in a strict, cloistered monastery. During the first few months I was there, I had a mystical experience of God as formless Divine Light.

But when I shared my experience with my superior, she thought I was too young to have such an experience, and so thought I was going crazy. I was asked to leave. I left, feeling misunderstood by the nuns and rejected by God. Later I questioned a number of priests and nuns about God appearing as Divine Light, but none could give me any guidance or support. They had no personal experiences to draw from. I felt totally forsaken by the Church.

Later research revealed to me that Christian mystics were many times ill-treated and were always highly suspect among those who believed rational thoughts about God were superior to personal ecstatic experiences of God.

Amma's life has taught me that mystical states of consciousness are usually misunderstood, and that one needs to be loving, patient, forgiving, and understanding to those who cannot comprehend them. She reaffirmed for me that a personal experience of God is what true spirituality is all about.

India's great spiritual gifts to the West have been her saints and sages, who have taught us methods of how to turn inward to our own souls, and to meditate deeply to find God's presence within us. Meditation is not a religion. It is a spiritual science of God-realization.

From witnessing the way Amma trains her monastics in renunciation, I was reminded once again that self-sacrifice is necessary for the attainment of the highest state of happiness—spiritual bliss.

Anyone studying for a career in medicine, science, art, or music, for example, knows that it takes intense years of training and self-sacrifice. But somehow regarding spiritual attainment, we in the West think we can achieve our goals effortlessly. We want to preserve our ego, have all our physical comforts met, and yet still awaken to the soul, the God within us.

Amma says that in spiritual life—where the ultimate gain is so much greater and far more precious than any material gain—it is necessary to renounce many pleasure-giving objects and material desires. When a devotee is mature enough, she said, those lower desires fall away by themselves, and there is no sense of sacrifice.

My experiences in India taught me much about sacrifice. I couldn't help but admire how hardworking and self-sacrificing Amma and her monastics are. Anyone who has traveled to India under rugged conditions knows that coming back to the United States is a culture shock.

Indian people are starving and striving for more material comforts. In contrast, the American people have more than enough material comforts, and a majority are overweight. India looks to the West for more efficient technologies and materialistic gains. But we turn to the East to learn from India's spiritual giants.

A balance is needed in this world between spirituality and materiality.

At the moment, the global mind-set has swung to the extreme left of rational materialism. It's like being on the ship *Titanic*—we are listing dangerously to one side—getting ready to sink.

Amma's force for good in the world is helping to bring us back into balance. If Amma does nothing more than she has already done, she will be remembered as a great humanitarian and one of the greatest healers and spiritual leaders in the history of religion.

GLOSSARY

ॐ

ASHRAM: "Place of striving." A place where spiritual seekers and aspirants live or visit in order to lead a spiritual life. It is usually the home of a spiritual master, saint, or ascetic who guides the aspirants in spiritual practices.

AUM: Sacred syllable. The Primordial Sound or Vibration, which represents Brahman and the entire creation. Aum is the primary mantra and is usually found at the beginning of other mantras.

AYURVEDA: "The science of life." Ancient holistic Indian health and medicinal system. Ayurvedic medicines are usually prepared from medicinal herbs and plants.

BHAGAVAD GITA: The teachings of Lord Krishna to Arjuna. It is a practical guide for common man for everyday life and is the essence of Vedic wisdom.

BHAJAN: Devotional singing.

BHAVA DARSHAN: The occasion when Amma receives devotees in the exalted state of the Divine Mother. In the early days, Amma also appeared in Krishna Bhava.

BRAHMACHARI(NI): A celibate disciple who practices spiritual disciplines and is usually being trained by a guru.

BRAHMAN: The Absolute Reality; the Whole; the Supreme Being, which encompasses and pervades everything and is One and indivisible.

DARSHAN: An audience with or a vision of the Divine or a holy person.

DEVI: "The Effulgent One." The Goddess.

DEVI BHAVA: "The Divine Mood of Devi." The state in which Amma reveals Her oneness and identity with the Divine Mother.

DHARMA: "That which upholds the universe." Dharma has many meanings, including the Divine Law, the law of existence in accordance with divine harmony, righteousness, religion, duty, responsibility, right conduct, justice, goodness, and truth. Dharma signifies the inner principles of religion.

DURGA: A name of Shakti, the Divine Mother. She is often depicted as wielding a number of weapons and riding a lion. She is the destroyer of evil and the protector of that which is good. She destroy the desires and negative tendencies (*vasanas*) of her children and unveils the Supreme Self.

GURU: "One who removes the darkness of ignorance." Spiritual master/guide.

KALI: "The Dark One." An aspect of the Divine Mother. From the viewpoint of the ego, She may seem frightening because She destroys the ego. But She destroys the ego and transforms us only out of Her immeasurable compassion. Kali has many forms; in Her benevolent form, She is known as Bhadra Kali. A devotee knows that behind Her fierce facade, the loving Mother is to be found, who protects Her children and bestows the grace of Liberation.

KRISHNA: "He who draws us to himself"; "the Dark One." The principal incarnation of Vishnu. He was born into a royal family, but grew up with foster parents and lived as a young cowherd in Vrindavan, where he was loved and worshipped by his devoted companions, the *gopis* and *gopas*. Krishna later became the ruler of Dwaraka. He was a friend of and adviser to his cousins, the Pandavas, especially Arjuna, to whom he revealed his teachings in the Bhagavad Gita.

KRISHNA BHAVA: The state in which Amma reveals Her oneness and identity with Krishna.

KUNDALINI: "The Serpent Power." The spiritual energy that rests like a coiled snake at the base of the spine. Through spiritual practices it is made to rise through the sushumna canal, a subtle nerve within the spine, and move up through the chakras (power centers). As the kundalini rises from chakra to chakra, the spiritual aspirant begins to experience finer levels of consciousness. The kundalini finally reaches the highest chakra at the top of the head (the Sahasrara Lotus), which leads to Liberation.

MAHATMA: "Great soul." When Amma uses the word *mahatma*, She is referring to a Self-realized soul.

MANTRA: Sacred formula or prayer that is constantly repeated. This awakens one's dormant spiritual powers and helps one to reach the goal. It is most effective if received from a spiritual master during initiation.

MUDRA: A sign by hand indicating mystic spiritual truths.

PRASAD: The consecrated offerings distributed after puja. Whatever a mahatma gives as a sign of his blessing is considered *prasad*.

PUJA: Worship.

RISHI: A great sage or seer.

SAMADHI: *Sam* = "with"; *adhi* = "the Lord." Oneness with God. A state of deep, one-pointed concentration, in which all thoughts subside and the mind enters into a state of complete stillness in which only Pure Consciousness remains, as one abides in the Atman (Self.)

SARI: A long piece of cloth worn by Indian ladies.

SHAKTI: The dynamic aspect of the Universal Mother.

SHIVA/SIVA: The static aspect of Brahman as the male principle.

SWAMI/NI: A monk or nun who has taken formal vows of renunciation and wears a traditional ochre-colored cloth representing the burning away of all attachments.

UPANISHADS: The concluding portion of the Vedas dealing with the philosophy of nondualism.

VEDA: "Knowledge, Wisdom." The ancient, sacred scriptures of

Hinduism. A collection of holy texts in Sanskrit that are divided into four parts: Rig, Yajur, Sama, and Atharva. They are among the world's oldest scriptures. The Vedas are considered to be the direct revelation of the Supreme Truth, which God bestowed upon the rishis.

VEDANTA: The philosophy of the Upanishads, the concluding part of the Vedas, which holds the Ultimate Truth to be "One without a Second."

YOGA: "To unite." A series of methods through which one can attain oneness with the Divine. A path that leads to Self-realization.

YOGI: Someone who is established in the practice of yoga, or is established in union with the Supreme Spirit.

NOTES

ༀ

PROLOGUE

New York City, July 15, 1999
The prologue was constructed from interviews with the police officers William La Pough and Juan Colon, and *New York Times*
reporter Corey Kilgannon and Corey's unpublished notes.

PART 1

In Part 1 (chapters 1 through 6) the historic narrative for Amma's
early life is derived from the following primary resources:
- 1999 taped interviews by author while in India of: Amma, her parents, sister Kasturi, villagers, and a number of the monastics who
  had been with her over twenty years.
- 1997 video transcripts of interviews with Amma, her parents and
  relatives by Dharmic Productions (Sridhar and Kripa Silberfein)
  and Shawn Brinsfield.
- Unpublished notes from Shawn Brinsfield's 1998 interviews with
  Amma's grandparents, family members, villagers, and third-grade
  school teacher.
- Swami Amritaswarupananda's English translation and adaptation of
  the original Indian biography: *AMMACHI: A Biography of Mata
  Amritanandamayi* (San Ramon: Mata Amritanandamayi Center,

1994.) It covers Amma's early years through 1983. It includes a few other healing stories not mentioned in this present biography.

The following books were also referenced:

Fuller, Sir Bampflyde. *Studies of Indian Life and Sentiment.* John Murray Publishers, London, 1917.

Kusy, Frank. *India.* The Globe Pequot Press, Chester, Connecticut, 1987, 2nd edition.

Wolpert, Stanley. *India.* University of California Press, Berkeley, 1991.

CHAPTER 1:

The following resources were used for a summary understanding of the Hindu gods Krishna and Vishnu, and the goddess Kali:

Harding, Elizabeth U. *Kali: The Black Goddess of Dakshinewar.* Nicolas-Hays, Inc., York Beach, Maine, 1993.

Vanamali. *The Play of God: Visions of the Life of Krishna.* Blue Dove Press, San Diego, 1998.

Pattanaik, Devdutt. *Vishnu: An Introduction.* Vakils, Feffer and Simons Ltd., Mumbai, India, 1998.

CHAPTER 2:

In addition to an interview with Dr. David Frawley, the director of the American Institute of Vedic Sciences, the following article was referenced:

Hochschild, Adam. "South India: Kerala-Land of Marx and Maharajahs." In *San Francisco Examiner Magazine*, Sunday, July 18, 1999. (This article was excerpted from his award-winning, nonfiction book, *King Leopold's Ghost: A Story of Greed, Terror and Heroism in Colonial Africa.*)

CHAPTER 3:

The following resource was used for understanding the subtle but definite laws by which the great Indian yogis and saints perform miracles:

Yogananda, Paramahansa. *Autobiography of a Yogi*. Self-Realization
   Fellowship, Los Angeles, 1990, 12th edition, pp. 360–61.

CHAPTER 4:

Dr. Jim Ryan was interviewed as an expert in Asian religious tradi-
tions. Professor Ryan has been to India numerous times and has met
Amma and other Indian saints.
In addition the following references were used:
Trebay, Guy. "Hindu Holy Woman Heals with Hugs." *The Village
   Voice*, July 15–21, 1998.
Amritaswarupananda, Swami. *Awaken Children*, part 1, Mata Amri-
   tanandamayi Center, San Ramon, 1989, pp. 81–84. Amma ex-
   plains Kundalini Shakti.
http://www.padrepio.com. This site for the Padre Pio Foundation in
   America contains an article titled, "Padre Pio's Cell." This arti-
   cle mentions the use of a horse thermometer to take Padre Pio's
   temperature.
Ruffin, C. Bernard. *Padre Pio: The True Story*. Our Sunday Visitor,
   Huntington, Indiana, 1991.

CHAPTER 5:

The following references were used:
Amritaswarupananda, Swami. *Awaken Children*, vol. 7, Mata Amri-
   tanandamayi Center, San Ramon, 1995, pp. 93–94.
Sri, S. Shankaranarayanan. *Sri Chakra*. Dipti Publications, Madras,
   India, 1979.
Head, Joseph, and Cranston, S. L., eds. *Reincarnation: The Phoenix
   Fire Mystery*. Julian Press/Crown Publishers, Inc., New York, 1978.

CHAPTER 6:

The following resources were used:
Amritaprana, Swamini. *Matruvani Magazine*, part 28, September
   1994, Amritapuri Ashram, India.

Amritaswarupananda, Swami. *Awaken Children*, vol. 6, Mata Amritanandmayi Center, San Ramon, 1994, pp. 162–64.

———. *Awaken Children*, part 1, Mata Amritanandamayi Center, San Ramon, 1989, pp. 260–63.

Paramatmananda, Swami. *On the Road to Freedom: A Pilgrimage in India*, vol. 1, Mata Amritanandamayi Center, San Ramon, 1997.

Sreekumar (Swami Poornamritananda). "Reminiscences." In *Immortal Bliss*, 2nd quarter, Mata Amritanandamayi Center, San Ramon, 1992.

http://www.who.int/lep/ (a website on Leprosy)

CHAPTER 7:

This chapter was structured using interviews from Calliope Karvounis, Brahmachari Shubamrita, Swami Paramatmananda, Meenakshi, Swami Ramakrishnananda, Swamini Krishnamritaprana, Swamini Amritaprana, Dr. Ragavan, M.D., and Dr. Dave, Ph.D., including the following resources:

Amritaswarupananda, Swami. *Awaken Children*, vol. 7, Mata Amritanandamayi Center, San Ramon, 1995.

———. *Awaken Children*, vol. 9, Mata Amritanandamayi Center, San Ramon, 1998.

PART 2

CHAPTER 8:

This chapter was created using notes from the author's visits to Amma's numerous charities and interviews with: Swamini Krishnamritaprana, Swami Abhayamrita Chaitanya, Amma's parents and villagers Samban and Manorama, and Remya, the director of charities. The following article and books were also referenced:

Sneha. "Great Undertakings: Amrita Institute of Technology and Science." In *Amritanandam*, 4th quarter, 1997, vol. 12, no. 4, Mata Amritanadamyi Center, San Ramon, pp. 16–27.

Amritaswarupananda, Swami. *Awaken Children*, part 1. Mata Amritanandamayi Center, San Ramon, 1989, pp. 89–90. Amma speaks about the advantage of meditation for children.

———. *Awaken Children*, vol. 8, Mata Amritanandamayi Center, San Ramon, 1996, pp. 110–13. Amma talks about the importance of relaxation as a method for learning any subject well.

Chapter 9:

This chapter incorporates author's interviews with: Amma, Brahmachari Shakti Prasad, Swami Paramatmananda, Swami Turiyamritananda, Dr. David Frawley, and author's notes on the new temple installation in Palakkad, India.

Other resources included:

Amritanandamayi Devi, Sri Mata. "The Status and Role of Women in Society Today." In *Matruvani Magazine*, Malayalam editions; October, November, December, 1996 and January, February, March, 1997, Amritapuri Ashram, India.

———. *The Brahmasthanam: An Epoch-Making Temple*. Mata Amritanandamayi Math, Amritapuri Ashram, India, 1995 edition.

Amritaswarupananda, Swami. *Awaken Children*, part 1, Mata Amritanandamayi Center, San Ramon, 1989.

———. *Awaken Children*, vol. 3, Mata Amritanandamayi Center, San Ramon, 1991.

———. *Awaken Children*, vol. 9, Mata Amritanandamayi Center, San Ramon, 1998, pp. 150–51.

Campbell, Joseph. *Myths to Live By*. Bantam Books, New York, 1988.

Frawley, David. *Gods, Sages and Kings: Vedic Secrets of Ancient Civilization*. Passage Press, Salt Lake City, Utah, 1991, pp. 258–62.

Nayak, B. U., and Ghosh, N. C. *The New Trends in Indian Art and Archaeology*. Aditya Prakashan, New Delhi, 1992.

Rajaram, Nayarantna, and Frawley, David. *Vedic Aryans and the Origins of Civilization: A Literary and Scientific Perspective*. World Heritage Press, Ottawa and New Delhi, 1994.

Dr. David Frawley's website, http://hindubooks.org/david_frawley/myth_aryan_invasion/, is quite informative on the ancient Vedic tradition and the current controversies concerning the Aryan invasions.

CHAPTER 10:

This chapter was created using the author's interviews with Dr. William Gough, president of the Foundation for Mind-Being Research, Dr. I. C. Dave, Dr. D. N. Srivastava, Dr. I. V. V. Raghavacharyulu, and the following resources:

Amritaswarupananda, Swami. *Awaken Children*, vol. 5, Mata Amritanandamayi Center, San Ramon, 1993, pp. 16–18.

Jitatmananda, Swami. *Modern Physics and Vedanta*. Bharatiya Vidya Bhavan, Bombay, India, 1992.

Pillai, Dr. Chandrasekhara. "Amma-Super Physicist." In *Amritanandam*, 1st quarter, 1996, vol. 11, no. 1, Mata Amritanandamayi Center, San Ramon, pp. 28–34.

Srivastava, Dr. D. N. "The Origin of Order in Nature." In *Maeer's MIT Pune Journal*, vol. 3, November 1994–January 1995.

Of Sound Mind and Body. Video. Macromedia, Epping, New Hampshire.

Jenny, Hans. *Cymatics*, German ed., Basilius Presses, Basel, Switzerland, 1974, p. 100.

Yogananda, Paramahansa. "My Mother's Death and the Mystic Amulet." In *Autobiography of a Yogi*. Self-Realization Fellowship, Los Angeles, 1990, 12th edition, pp. 16–23.

Zimmer, Heinrich. *Artistic Form and Yoga in the Sacred Images of India*. Princeton University Press, Princeton, N.J., 1990 edition.

CHAPTER 11:

This chapter was constructed using interviews with Meenaski, Swamini Amritaprana, Ramana, Hari Suda, Louise Pare, Judy Walter, Dr. Michael Flanagin, Dr. I. C. Dave, Francis Rame, Lucia Birnbaum, Georgia Kelly, and Olga Luchakova, M.D., Ph.D., along with the following magazine article, books, and websites:

Nalini. "Russia Is Cradled in Mother's Arms." In *Amritanandam*,

3rd quarter, 1991, Mata Amritananadamayi Center, San Ramon, pp. 44–47.

Amritaswarupananda, Swami. *Awaken Children*, vol. 6, Mata Amritanandamayi Center, San Ramon, 1994, pp. 159–61.

Begg, Ean. *The Cult of the Black Virgin*. Penquin Books, London, 1996.

Birnbaum, Lucia Chiavola. *Black Madonnas: Feminism, Religion, and Politics in Italy*. Northeastern University Press, Boston, 1993.

Cornell, Judith. *Mandala: Luminous Symbols for Healing*. Quest Books, Wheaton, Ill., 1994, pp. 140–49.

Du Boulay, Shirley. *A Biography of Bede Griffiths: Beyond the Darkness*. Doubleday, New York, 1998, pp. 228–32.

Galland, China. *Longing for Darkness: Tara and the Black Madonna*. Viking/Penquin, New York, 1990, p. 295.

Harding, Elizabeth U. *Kali: The Black Goddess of Dakshinewar*. Nicolas-Hays, Inc., York Beach, Maine, 1993.

Jung, C. G. *Man and His Symbols*. Doubleday & Company, New York, 1964.

Woodman, Marion, and Dickson, Elinor. *Dancing in the Flames: The Dark Goddess in the Transformation of Consciousness*. Shambhala, Boston, 1997.

The following resources were used for Our Lady of Fatima:

Gale-Kumar, Kristina. *The Scriptures Are Fulfilled*. Cardinal Interprises, Karnataka, India, 1991.

Zimdars-Swartz, Sandra L. *Encountering Mary*. Avon Books, New York, 1991.

Lucia and a number of other Catholics do not consider the pope's 1984 dedication of Russia valid because not all bishops participated nor did the pope use the word *Russia* in his dedication — see websites below.

http://www.fatima.org/core.html (a website on Our Lady of Fatima)
http://www.fatima.org/weop/e7cp4.html

The following websites were used for a summary overview of Russian and Byzantine history:

http://www.departments.bucknell.edu/russian/history.htm

A huge resource and link page for pre/post 1917 Russian history:
http://members.aol.com/AACTchrOz/russia.html

For information on Russian culture—holy icons:
http://russianculture.about.com/msub22.htm
http://www.decani.yunet.com/history.html
http://www.wsu.edu:8080~dee/MA/BYZ.HTM

CHAPTER 12:

This chapter was constructed from interviews with Amma, Dr. Prem Nair, Sneha (Karen Mo), Ron Gottsegen, and Swami Amritaswarupananda, in addition to the following resources:

Saradananda, Swami. *Sri Ramakrishna the Great Master.* English translation by Swami Jagadananda, Sri Ramakrishna Math, Mylapore, Madras, India, pp. 160–63.

"The Miracle of AIMS." In *Immortal Bliss*, 3rd quarter, 1998, vol. 12, no. 3, Mata Amritanandamayi Center, San Ramon, pp. 12–21.

Nair, Prem, M.D. "AMMA Is My Life." In *Immortal Bliss*, 3rd quarter, 1998, vol. 12, no. 3, Mata Amritanandamayi Center, San Ramon, pp. 25–29.

CHAPTER 13:

This chapter was assembled using interviews with Stephen Bodian, Swami Paramatmananda, Swami Shraddhananda Saraswati, Sister Rose Mercurio, Darsana, Cindy, Victoria, Janani, and Ramana and the following book:

Amritaswarupananda, Swami. *Awaken Children*, vol. 5, Mata Amritanandamayi Center, San Ramon, 1993, pp. 59–61.

——. *Awaken Children*, vol. 7, Mata Amritanandamayi Center, San Ramon, 1995, pp. 183–88. Amma's teaching regarding false gurus.

CHAPTER 14:

This chapter was constructed from the author's notes of the North India tour and interviews with Amma, Priyan, Jani, Swami Ramakrishnananda, and Sri Pati, including the following resource:

Pagels, Elaine. *The Gnostic Gospels*. Vintage Books, New York, 1981, pp. 58–59.

EPILOGUE

Yogananada, Paramahansa. "Rabindranath Tagore and I Compare Schools." In *Autobiography of a Yogi*. Self-Realization Fellowship, Los Angeles, 1987, pp. 259–63.

BIBLIOGRAPHY

Amritaswarupananda, Swami. *A Biography of Mata Amritanandamayi*, Kerala, India: Mata Amritanandamayi Mission Trust, 1988.

———. *Awaken Children*, part 1, San Ramon: Mata Amritanandamayi Center, 1989.

———. *Awaken Children*, part 2, San Ramon: Mata Amritanandamayi Center, 1991.

———. *Awaken Children*, vol. 3, San Ramon: Mata Amritanandamayi Center, 1991.

———. *Awaken Children*, vol. 4, San Ramon: Mata Amritanandamayi Center, 1992.

———. *Awaken Children*, vol. 5, San Ramon: Mata Amritanandamayi Center, 1993.

———. *Awaken Children*, vol. 6, San Ramon: Mata Amritanandamayi Center, 1994.

———. *Awaken Children*, vol. 7, San Ramon: Mata Amritanandamayi Center, 1995.

———. *Awaken Children*, vol. 8, San Ramon: Mata Amritanandamayi Center, 1996.

———. *Awaken Children*, vol. 9, San Ramon: Mata Amritanandamayi Center, 1998.

Begg, Ean. *The Cult of the Black Virgin*. London: Penguin Books, 1996.

Birnbaum, Lucia Chiavola. *Black Madonnas: Feminism, Religion, and Politics in Italy*. Boston: Northeastern University Press, 1993.

Campbell, Joseph. *Myths to Live by*. New York: Bantam Books, 1988.

Cornell, Judith. *Mandala: Luminous Symbols for Healing*. Wheaton, Il.: Quest Books, 1994.

Cottler, Marty, ed. *Come Quickly My Darling Children!: Stories by Western Devotees of Mata Amritanandamayi*. Grass Valley, Cal: Sierra Vista Publishing, 1996.

Du Boulay, Shirley. *A Biography of Bede Griffiths: Beyond the Darkness*. New York: Doubleday, 1998.

Ehrich, Robert W., ed. *Chronologies in Old World Archaeology*. 3rd ed., vol. 1, Chicago: University of Chicago Press, 1992.

Frawley, Dr. David. *Gods, Sages, and Kings: Vedic Secrets of Ancient Civilization*. Salt Lake City, Utah: Passage Press, 1991.

———. *Tantric Yoga and the Wisdom Goddesses*. Salt Lake City, Utah: Passage Press, 1996.

Gale-Kumar, Kristina. *The Scriptures Are Fulfilled*. Karnataka, India: Cardinal Interprises, 1991.

Galland, China. *Longing for Darkness: Tara and the Black Madonna*. New York: Viking/Penguin, 1990.

Harding, Elizabeth U. *Kali: The Black Goddess of Dakshinewar*. York Beach, Maine: Nicolas-Hays, Inc., 1993.

Jenny, Hans. *Cymatics*. German ed. Basel, Switzerland: Basilius Presses, 1974.

Jitatmananda, Swami. *Modern Physics and Vedanta*. Bombay, India: Bharatiya Vidya Bhavan, 1992.

Jnanamritananda Puri, Swami, ed. *Eternal Wisdom, Upadeshamritam*, vol. 1. San Ramon: Mata Amritanandamayi Center, 1997.

———. *Eternal Wisdom, Upadeshamritam*, vol. 2, San Ramon: Mata Amritanandamayi Center, 1999.

Jung, C. G. *Man and His Symbols*. New York: Doubleday & Company, 1964.

Nayak, B. U., and Ghosh, N. C. *The New Trends in Indian Art and Archaeology*. New Delhi: Aditya Prakashan, 1992.

Pagels, Elaine. *The Gnostic Gospels*. New York: Vintage Books, 1981.

Paramatmananda, Swami. *On the Road to Freedom*, vol. 1, San Ramon: Mata Amritanandaymayi Center, 1987.

Pattanaik, Devdutt. *Vishnu: An Introduction*. Mumbai, India: Vakils, Feffer and Simons Ltd., 1998.

Pole, Karuna. *Getting to Joy: A Western Householder's Spiritual Journey with Mata Amritanandamayi*. Seattle, Wash.: Shantini Center, 1997.

Radha, Sivanada Swami. *Kundalini Yoga for the West*. Boulder, Colo. Shambhala Publications, 1978.

Rajaram, Nayarantna, and Frawley, David. *Vedic Aryans and the Origins of Civilization: A Literary and Scientific Perspective*. Ottawa and New Delhi: World Heritage Press, 1994.

Rao, S. R. *Dawn and Evolution of the Indus Civiliation*. New Delhi: Aditya Prakashan, 1992.

Ruffin, C. Bernard. *Padre Pio: The True Story*. Huntington: Our Sunday Visitor, 1991.

Saradananda, Swami. *Sri Ramakrishna the Great Master*. English translation by Swami Jagadananda, Madras, India: Sri Ramakrishna Math, *n.d.*

Shankaranarayanan. *Sri Chakra*. Pondicherry, India: Dipti Publications, 1979.

Vanamali. *The Play of God: Visions of the Life of Krishna*. San Diego, Cal.: Blue Dove Press, 1998.

Srivastava, Dr. D. N. "The Origin of Order in Nature." Maeer's *MIT Pune Journal*, vol. 3; November 1994–January 1995.

Yogananada, Paramahansa. *Autobiography of a Yogi*. Los Angeles: Self-Realization Fellowship, 1987.

———. *The Bhagavad Gita: Royal Science of God-Realization*, vols. 1 and 2, Los Angeles: Self-Realization Fellowship, 1995.

Zeff, Ted. *Searching for God: A Journey into the Divine Mother*. San Ramon: Shiva Publications, 1997.

Zimdars-Swartz, Sandra L. *Encountering Mary*. New York: Avon Books, 1991.

Zimmer, Heinrich. *Artistic Form and Yoga in the Sacred Images of India*. Princeton, N.J.: Princeton University Press, 1990.

MAGAZINES

Immortal Bliss, 1st and 2nd quarters, 1999, 3rd and 4th quarters, 1998, Mata Amritanandamayi Center, San Ramon.

Amritananadam, 4th quarter, 1997, 1st, 2nd, and 4th quarters, 1996, 1st and 2nd quarters, 1995, 3rd and 4th quarters, 1994, 4th quarter, 1992, Mata Amritanandamayi Center, San Ramon.

Mata Amritanandamayi. "The Status and Role of Women in Society Today." In *Matruvani* Indian Malayalam serial editions; October, November, December, 1996 and January, February, March, 1997.

Hochschild, Adam. "South India: Kerala-Land of Marx and Maharajahs." In *San Francisco Examiner Magazine*, Sunday, July 18, 1999.

APPENDIX

LEARN MORE ABOUT AMMA

UNITED KINGDOM

Contact the MA Center. Details below

UNITED STATES

Mata Amritanandamayi Center (MA Center)
P.O. Box 613
San Ramon, CA 94583-0613
Phone (510) 537-9417
Fax (510) 889-8585
E-mail: macenter@ammachi.org

Visit website: www.ammachi.org for more complete information on Amma's retreats, world tours, ashrams, and other centers around the world.
Other websites: www.amma.fi (Finland); www.ammachi.org.au (Australia); www.amma.nu (Sweden); www.pcug.co.uk (United Kingdom); www.amma.de (official site for Europe in English, German, French, and Dutch)

Visit website: www.mothersbooks.org for meditation accessories, *Awaken Children* books, music tapes of Amma and her swamis chanting, multimedia CDs and videos of Amma on her various world tours. For a paper catalog of books and tapes, write to the Mata Amritanandamayi Center (MA Center) at the above address. All proceeds go to support Amma's charities.

The San Ramon Ashram publishes *Immortal Bliss,* a quarterly journal dedicated to Amma and her teachings. To subscribe contact the MA Center.

INDIA

Mata Amritanandamayi Math
Amritapuri P.O., Kollam Dt.
Kerala 690 525 India
Phone 91 (476) 621-279
      91 (476) 897-578
Fax   91 (476) 897-678
E-mail: inform@amritapuri.org

The Amritapuri Ashram publishes a monthly magazine called *Matruvani* that is dedicated to Amma and her teachings. It is published in numerous languages, including English.
For subscription information, write to:
The Publisher, *Matruvani*
Amritapuri P.O., Kollam Dt.
Kerala 690 525 India
Or you can E-mail: inform@amritapuri.org

(AIMS) The Amrita Institute of Medical Sciences and Research Center
For information on the AIMS Hospital project for volunteering or donating funds contact:
Karen Moawad, Director of Development (Circle of Compassion Campaign)
The AIMS Project
P.O. Box 10279
Bainbridge Island, WA 98110
E-mail: KarenMo@aol.com
Visit website: www.aimsproject.org

INDEX